T0246727

SECRET
# STOCKHOLM

*Per Faxneld*

JONGLEZ PUBLISHING

Travel guides

**W**e immensely enjoyed writing the *Secret Stockholm* guide and hope that, like us, you will continue to discover the unusual, secret and lesser-known facets of this city. Accompanying the description of some sites, you will find historical information and anecdotes that will let you understand the city in all its complexity.

*Secret Stockholm* also sheds light on the numerous yet overlooked details of places we pass by every day. These details are an invitation to pay more attention to the urban landscape and, more generally, to regard our city with the same curiosity and attention we often feel when travelling ...

Comments on this guide and its contents, as well as information on sites not mentioned, are welcome and will help us to enrich future editions.

Don't hesitate to contact us:
Email: info@jonglezpublishing.com

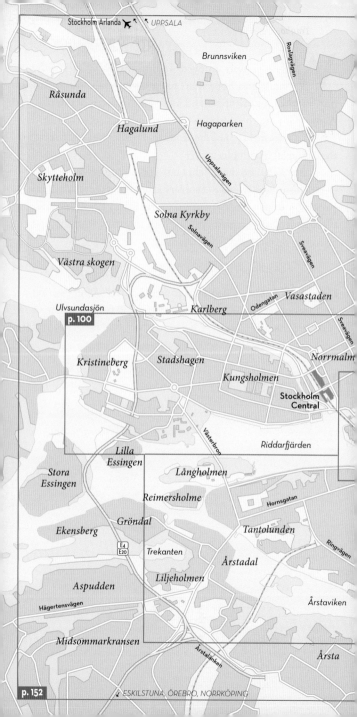

Stockholm Arlanda ✈  ↗ UPPSALA

Brunnsviken

Råsunda

Hagalund

Hagaparken

Skytteholm

Uppsalavägen

Solna Kyrkby

Solnavägen

Sveavägen

Västra skogen

Vasastaden

Ulvundasjön
**p. 100**

Karlberg

Odengatan

Kristineberg

Stadshagen

Norrmalm

Kungsholmen

Sveavägen

**Stockholm Central**

Västerbron

Riddarfjärden

Lilla Essingen

Stora Essingen

Långholmen

Reimersholme

Hornsgatan

Ekensberg

Gröndal

Tantolunden

E4 E20

Trekanten

Årstadal

Ringvägen

Aspudden

Liljeholmen

Hägertensvägen

Årstaviken

Midsommarkransen

Årstalänken

Årsta

**p. 152**

⚓ ESKILSTUNA, ÖREBRO, NORRKÖPING

p. 234

Tranholmen

Islinge

Torsvik

Norra Kungsvägen

Lidingo

Lilla Värtan

Norra
Djurgården

Herserud

Lidingöbron

Baggeby

Södra Kungsvägen

Hjorthagen

E20

Lidingövägen

Ladugårdsgärdet

Valhallavägen

Lindarängsvägen

Sturegatan

Östermalm

p. 10

Strandvägen

Vasamuseet

Skeppsholmen

Djurgården

Gamla
Stan

**STOCKHOLM**

Saltsjön

Danviken

Värmdöleden

Södermalm

Henriksdal

Finntorp

Götgatan

Värmdövägen

Alphyddan

Södra
Hammarbyhmanen

p. 66

Björkhagen

Ninäsvägen

N

0          1          2 km

# CONTENTS

## *Gamla Stan*

| | |
|---|---|
| FAUN AND VULVA ORNAMENT | *12* |
| *THE FAMILY* STATUE'S ROTATING FEATURE | *14* |
| THE CANNON-FLANKED DOOR OF VÄSTERLÅNGGATAN 68 | *16* |
| MÅRTEN TROTZIGS GRÄND | *20* |
| PLAQUE OF CARL LARSSON'S BIRTHPLACE | *22* |
| BLACK FRIARS' CELLAR | *24* |
| THE RELIEF OF HUSET BRASAN | *26* |
| THE BURNT LOT | *28* |
| THE ROSE DOOR | *30* |
| DRAYMEN'S GUILD ROOMS | *32* |
| ANCKARSTRÖM'S GUNS IN THE ROYAL ARMOURY | *34* |
| OLD PUBLIC URINAL | *36* |
| IRON BOY SCULPTURE | *38* |
| 92 BLOODBATH STONES | *40* |
| CANNONBALL IN THE WALL | *44* |
| THE RUNE STONE CORNER | *46* |
| FIRST-GENERATION PHONE BOOTH | *48* |
| HUSET KRONAN | *50* |
| THE PETRIFIED CAT BAS-RELIEF | *52* |
| GÅSGRÄND | *54* |
| HELL ALLEY | *56* |
| CROSSED-OUT PLOMMENFELT FAMILY CREST | *58* |
| SLIDES OF THE OLD NATIONAL ARCHIVE | *62* |
| MEDUSA HEAD IN RIDDARHOLMSKYRKAN | *64* |

## *Sodermalm*

| | |
|---|---|
| SKANSTULL CHOLERA GRAVEYARD | *68* |
| JULIUS HUS | *70* |
| KATARINA FIRE STATION LANTERN | *72* |
| THE DECORATION OF THE COPPER DOORS OF ÖSTGÖTAGATAN 14 | *74* |
| THE CRACKS OF THE BELL OF KATARINA CHURCH | *76* |
| ERSTA COMMUNION WAFER BAKERY | *78* |
| TEATER DUR OCH MOLL | *80* |

CAPTAIN ROLLA MONUMENT                              82
THE BELLMAN HOUSE                                   84
THE ALMGREN FACTORY                                 88
MERMAID STATUES AT THE VAN DER NOOT PALACE          92
JAS 39 GRIPEN CRASH MEMORIAL                        94
MINIATURE REPLICA OF MICKES SERIER, CD & VINYL      96
REIMERSHOLME VODKA BENCHES                          98

## Kungsholm – Normalm

LILLA HORNSBERG                                    102
ARONSBERG JEWISH CEMETERY                          104
INTERIOR OF ST GÖRANS GYMNASIUM                    106
THE VESTIGES OF THE FORMER BIOGRAF DRAKEN
CINEMA                                             108
SVEN HEDIN'S HOUSE                                 110
THE COLLECTIVE HOUSE                               114
AIRSHAFTS OF THE KRONOBERG REMAND PRISON           116
COPPER FACES OF RÅDHUSET                           118
PIPERSKA MUREN GARDEN                              122
JUGENDSTIL DOORS OF GASVERKET                      124
MUSEUM OF PHARMACEUTICAL HISTORY                   126
SKANDIA CINEMA                                     128
FENIXPALATSET                                      130
THE RELIEFS OF CENTRUMHUSET                        132
UGGLAN PHARMACY                                    136
THE RELIEFS OF CENTRALPOSTHUSET                    138
THE PHANTOM STATUE                                 140
THE SECRETS OF ADELSWÄRD HOUSE                     142
KUNGSTRÄDGÅRDEN METRO STATION                      144
RÖDA RUMMET AT BERNS                               150

## North-West

INSCRIPTION IN THE BRUNKEBERGSTUNNELN             154
SWEDENBORG CHURCH                                  156
LODGE OF THE KNIGHTS TEMPLAR                       160
THE GHOST CASTLE'S COLLECTION                      162

# CONTENTS

THE STORYTELLING ROOM ................................ 170
ANTHROPOSOPHICAL LIBRARY ......................... 172
THE EASTMAN INSTITUTE ............................... 176
GARDEN OF THE SENSES ................................. 178
SABBATSBERGS KYRKA .................................. 180
THE ALLEY UNDER ST ERIKSBRON .................... 182
THE GRAVE OF POMPE .................................. 184
STONE OF THE HIGH COUNCIL ........................ 186
THE KARLBERG RUNESTONE ........................... 188
ST. MATTEUS PARISH LIBRARY .......................... 190
BUDO ZEN CENTER ..................................... 192
FÖRENINGEN FÖR FÄKTKONSTENS FRÄMJANDE (FFF) 194
MONICA ZETTERLUND PARK ........................... 196
VILLA BELLONA .......................................... 198
VICTORIAVÄXTHUSET ................................... 200
WITTROCK TOWER ...................................... 202
CARL ELDH STUDIO MUSEUM .......................... 204
MESSENGER PIGEON CLUB ............................. 206
QUEEN CHRISTINA'S GAZEBO .......................... 208
HAGSTRÖMER MEDICO-HISTORICAL LIBRARY ........ 210
TURKISH KIOSK .......................................... 214
CHINESE PAVILION AT HAGA PARK ................... 216
CAVE AND PUMP SHAFT AT HAGA PARK ............. 218
HAGA CASTLE RUIN ..................................... 220
THE MONTELIUS GRAVE ................................ 222
HAGALUNDSPARKEN WATER TOWER ................. 224
OLLE OLSSON HOUSE MUSEUM ...................... 228
FILMSTADEN ............................................. 232

## North-East

KAKNÄS PET CEMETERY ................................ 236
THE EYE ON FILMHUSET ................................ 238
ITALIENSKA KULTURINSTITUTET ....................... 240
VILLA LUSTHUSPORTEN ................................. 242
SKÅNSKA GRUVAN ..................................... 244
BIOLOGICAL MUSEUM .................................. 252

DC-3 79001 HUGIN MEMORIAL STONE                              *254*
WASA GARDEN                                                  *256*
JÄGARHYDDAN                                                  *258*
CAPTIVE VIKING STATUE                                        *260*
SWEDENBORG'S GAZEBO                                          *262*
GIRAFFE CRANE                                                *266*
SECRETS OF KASTELLHOLMEN                                     *268*
THE VIKING SHIP AT THE FORMER SCHOOL OF
NAVAL WARFARE                                                *270*
BÅÅTSKA PALATSET                                             *272*
'DEVIL'S BIBLE' IN THE ROYAL LIBRARY                         *278*
FORMER CZECHOSLOVAKIAN EMBASSY                               *280*
TEKNISKA HÖGSKOLAN METRO STATION                            *282*
HIDDEN TREASURES OF THE ROYAL INSTITUTE OF
TECHNOLOGY                                                   *288*
R1                                                          *292*
OWLS OF UGGLEVIKSKÄLLAN                                      *294*
FISKARTORPET                                                 *296*
EDELCRANTZ OCTAGONAL TOWER                                   *298*


ALPHABETICAL INDEX                                           *300*

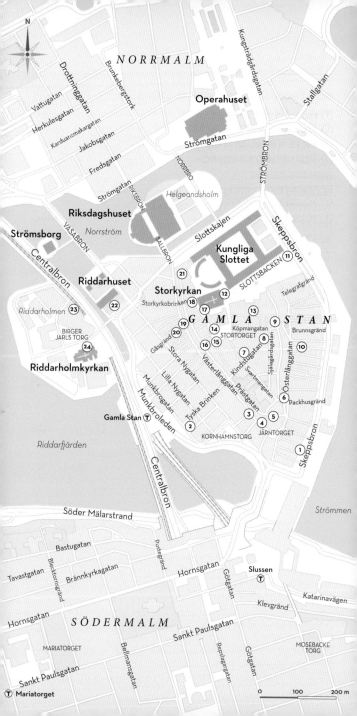

# Gamla Stan

1. FAUN AND VULVA ORNAMENT — *12*
2. *THE FAMILY* STATUE'S ROTATING FEATURE — *14*
3. THE CANNON-FLANKED DOOR OF VÄSTERLÅNGGATAN 68 — *16*
4. MÅRTEN TROTZIGS GRÄND — *20*
5. PLAQUE OF CARL LARSSON'S BIRTHPLACE — *22*
6. BLACK FRIARS' CELLAR — *24*
7. THE RELIEF OF HUSET BRASAN — *26*
8. THE BURNT LOT — *28*
9. THE ROSE DOOR — *30*
10. DRAYMEN'S GUILD ROOMS — *32*
11. ANCKARSTRÖM'S GUNS IN THE ROYAL ARMOURY — *34*
12. OLD PUBLIC URINAL — *36*
13. IRON BOY SCULPTURE — *38*
14. 92 BLOODBATH STONES — *40*
15. CANNONBALL IN THE WALL — *44*
16. THE RUNE STONE CORNER — *46*
17. FIRST-GENERATION PHONE BOOTH — *48*
18. HUSET KRONAN — *50*
19. THE PETRIFIED CAT BAS-RELIEF — *52*
20. GÅSGRÄND — *54*
21. HELL ALLEY — *56*
22. CROSSED-OUT PLOMMENFELT FAMILY CREST — *58*
23. SLIDES OF THE OLD NATIONAL ARCHIVE — *62*
24. MEDUSA HEAD IN RIDDARHOLMSKYRKAN — *64*

# FAUN AND VULVA ORNAMENT ①

*A weeping faun shedding tears onto genitalia?*

*Skeppsbron 44*
*Metro: Gamla stan*

A strange decoration on one of the Old Town houses facing the water has prompted much speculation. The building, erected in 1906, houses the restaurant Zum Franziskaner, which claims to be Stockholm's oldest, founded in 1421 (though it has, obviously, not been in the same location through the ages). Above the entrance to the door next to the restaurant, the horned and bearded face of a faun (a lustful human-goat hybrid in Graeco-Roman mythology) leers down at the street. Below him is what appears to be a vulva. At least, it has been interpreted as such by many. Those of a different opinion tend to stress that this would have been a surprisingly daring artistic choice in prudish turn-of-the-century Sweden.

It would not have been extremely far-fetched to couple a vulva with a faun, though, since fauns and the Greek god Pan are well-established as symbols of sexual freedom and debauchery in Swedish literature and art. Perhaps the sculptor put it there as an ambiguous joke, intended to confound those passers-by who were not only attentive but also had a dirty imagination. He might even have been asked to do so by his employer.

The house was commissioned by the wealthy Carl Smith (1822–1895), with architectural plans by Fredrik Dahlberg (1857–1932). Dr Katarina Bonnevier of the Stockholm School of Architecture, an authority on queer–feminist analyses of buildings, used to give guided tours of the city based on her special expertise. This house, designated 'fitthuset' (the cunt house) in some less polite circles, was among those included in her tour. Exactly how 'queer' the odd decoration is could perhaps be discussed, unless one assumes it is part of the faun's body, making him transsexual or a hermaphrodite.

According to some sources, people who work in the building tell a story that Carl Smith intended the vulva to symbolise his wife's infidelity. The male face above the ornament is mounted at an angle that supposedly makes it appear to be crying when it rains, thus shedding its tears down onto the vulva. Its weeping would indicate Smith's grief over his marital troubles. This story, though entertaining, seems a little implausible.

An equally fanciful explanation, but more occult, might be to take Bonnevier's queer line of argumentation in a different direction and link the faun face coupled with a vulva to French esotericist Eliphas Lévi's (1810–1875) famous image of Baphomet; this goatlike hermaphrodite symbolises the union of various opposites. To make such a reading fully convincing, evidence is needed of esoteric interests on the part of Smith, Dahlberg or the sculptor – which is unlikely.

# *THE FAMILY* STATUE'S ROTATING FEATURE

## Figures that can be moved around and even rotated

*Mälartorget*
*Metro: Gamla stan*

The statue *Familjen* (*The Family*) is close to the Old Town subway entrance and has a little-known feature and a dramatic recent past which is also largely obscure.

This bronze sculpture on a granite plinth depicts a mother, a father and their child. It is ingeniously constructed with tracks in the base, making it possible to move all three figures around and even rotate them. Anyone can rearrange the position of the family. Hence, one day the child can be moving away from its parents, and on the next it will be snugly embraced by them. And so on.

It is very rare to see someone actually manipulating the figures, though, since most people would assume a statue to be completely immobile.

The statue was made in 1972–73 by the sculptor Pye Engström (born in 1928), based on a smaller work she exhibited at an exhibition called Multikonst (*Multi Art*) in the 1960s. Engström specialises in pieces with a playful, inviting expression, often intended to be stroked and handled. She has commented that the sculptures benefit from being touched, and one aspect of this is that it adds to their patina.

## The stolen child

In November 2007, the family's child was, amazingly, stolen. The artist was devastated. She could not understand what anyone would want the child for and was baffled by how anyone could have removed it from the base. Today, the sculpture has been recreated by the artist and there is, again, a child sitting between the adults.

## Flies' Meeting: where the city's latrines were emptied

The square where the statue is located has a history stretching back at least to the mid-19th century and when it was used to unload agricultural wares coming in by boat. A less appealing but more colourful historical aspect of the location is that it was also previously the site where, behind a wooden fence, the city's latrines were emptied. The stinking mass was then taken away by boat by women who were often former prison inmates. Even though the square no longer fulfilled this function after the 1840s, the name associated with it – Flugmötet (*Flies' Meeting*) – lives on. It was even proposed as an official name in 1921, but the more neutral Mälartorget (Lake Mälaren Square) was chosen instead.

# THE CANNON-FLANKED DOOR OF VÄSTERLÅNGGATAN 68

## *The astonishing story of Descartes' skull and relics*

*Västerlånggatan 68*
*The interior of the house is not open to the public*
*Metro: Gamla stan*

The house at Västerlånggatan 68 is a striking example of baroque architecture, with the interesting addition of two cannon barrels flanking the door to the street. They are intended to protect the sculptures behind them from being damaged by passing carts and carriages and were added at the end of the 18th century.

The house itself was built on medieval foundations, around 1630, as the first of many private palaces during Sweden's Great Power period, eventually ending up as the residence of the French ambassador.

This is also where French philosopher René Descartes (1596–1650) died in 1650, in a possibly mysterious way (see following double page).

Man being stopped from entering the café located on the premises for many years. 1950s.
© Hernried, Karl Heinz/Nordiska museet

## Was Descartes poisoned by a Catholic priest?

In the biting winter month of January 1650, French philosopher René Descartes, then a guest at Swedish queen Kristina's court, caught a cold. By the beginning of February it turned into pneumonia, and he died from it on the 11th of that month. At the time, he was living with the French ambassador in his house on Västerlånggatan 68.

He had been invited by the queen to set up a scientific academy, and to provide her with private tutoring on his radical ideas about love and passions of the soul. The two did not get along, however, and the French guest did not enjoy his visits to Kristina's cold and draughty castle where she demanded the lessons start at five in the morning. According to Theodor Ebert – a Descartes specialist at the University of Erlangen – a Catholic missionary to Stockholm named Jacques Viogué had identified Descartes as a threat to hopes to convert the Swedish queen to Catholicism (which did happen later). Viogué and others considered Descartes' ideas heretical and a danger to a successful conversion.

The doctor who treated the philosopher found something wrong in his urine, which may have been a sign of poisoning. The fact that the patient himself – who was well-versed in medicine – asked for an emetic (to induce vomiting) also points in this direction. Neither of these things are consistent with the symptoms or treatment of pneumonia, but rather with arsenic poisoning. Ebert therefore suggests Descartes was assassinated by Viogué, using an arsenic-laced Holy Communion wafer. It could also be that the poison was administered in some other way.

During the 1908 restoration of the house, it was reported by the weekly *Idun* that the cellars, believed to be former monks' cells or dungeons, were found to contain secret passages running under the street outside. Perhaps Descartes' assassins, if they existed, gained access to the house through these passages and poisoned his food or drink?

After his death, Descartes was buried in Stockholm, but 16 years later he was exhumed by the new French ambassador, who was very keen on relics. Amazingly, he stole the philosopher's right index finger, which 'had served as an instrument for the universal writings of the deceased'. The bones, without the finger, were placed in a small copper casket and sent back to France but, unknown to all, the captain of the Swedish soldiers overseeing the opening of the grave stole the skull.

The remains were interred at the Sainte Geneviève church in Paris.

After further moves in conjunction with the 1789 Revolution (in which a heritage curator stole a flat bone to make rings for his friends!), in 1821 the French Academy oversaw an opening of the casket and discovered the skull was missing.

In one telling of the story, Swedish scientist Jöns Jacob Berzelius (1779–1848) heard of this, and when he saw that the skull was being auctioned in Stockholm, he bought it and finally repatriated the missing body part.

Was it the real skull? In total, five different skulls (one supposedly engraved with a poem in Latin and the names of nine successive owners) are attributed to Descartes …

# MÅRTEN TROTZIGS GRÄND

*Stockholm's most narrow alley, getting narrower by the year*

*The alley can be reached be reached from Prästgatan 80 or Västerlånggatan 79*
*Metro: Gamla stan*

Mårten Trotzigs gränd is Stockholm's most narrow alley. At its most narrow, it is 90 cm across. This narrowness makes it easy to miss. In some circles, a common cruel joke is to bring an obese person to Old Town, suggest a shortcut through Mårten Trotzigs gränd, and then watch the victim get stuck, ruin their clothes, or be forced to back out.

In the 1950s, the alley was where children would go to smoke cigarettes, while some of today's kids enjoy defacing its walls with graffiti.

A plaque in the alley states: 'Mårten Trotzig's alley / earlier known as narrow stairs alley / is named after the merchant Mårten Trotzig 1559–1617 / In August 1945 members of the Trotzig family installed this memorial plaque commemorating their ancestor'.

The plaque in fact predates (by four years) the official sanction being given for the name, which came only in 1949. In 1945 there were no stairs in the alley, and it was more or less just a dirt slope with some stones stuck in it. The walls of the houses on either side were badly worn and largely lacked plaster. The alley was restored and provided with a 36-step staircase.

Before 1945 the alley had been a truly secret place, seen only on old maps, since it was boarded up with planks on either side for 100 years, with no access.

Today the top of the alley (the top floor of the houses) is in danger of closing entirely at some points, since the houses are slowly sinking or collapsing inwards, making the space at the top a mere 50 cm across or so. This can be clearly seen on the streetlamp fixed to one wall, which now almost touches the opposite wall. If nothing is done, in a generation's time this will probably be a tunnel rather than an alley.

---

Then known as Herr Traubtzich, Mårten Trotzig immigrated to Sweden from Germany in 1581. His escutcheon (heraldic weapon) was decorated with grapes (*Trauben* in German), and later he changed his name to the more Swedish-sounding Trotzig (which sounds similar both to the word for 'defiant' in modern Swedish and to his heraldic insignia).

His business thrived in Sweden and he made a fortune in the copper trade, becoming one of the city's richest men. He bought the houses on both sides of the alley in 1597 and 1599, respectively. Trotzig's life ended dramatically when he was murdered on a business trip to Falun, north of Stockholm.

# PLAQUE OF CARL LARSSON'S BIRTHPLACE

⑤

*The dark past of the sunniest of Swedish painters*

*Prästgatan 78*
*Interior not open to the public*
*Metro: Gamla stan*

Swedish painter Carl Larsson's (1853–1919) work has in many ways come to epitomise Swedish national Romanticism. His technically immaculate coloured line drawings, oil paintings and other works are the sort of art the public usually loves – and art critics detest.

The same goes for his house in Sundborn, Dalarna, a *Gesamtkunstwerk* creation by Carl and his wife Karin along the lines of the ideals propounded by the British Arts and Crafts Movement. The plaque identifying the house in Old Town where he was born is easy to miss, especially since the wall has repeatedly been defaced with massive amounts of graffiti.

Carl's visual portrayals of life at Sundborn are famous for their harmonious, joyful atmosphere. When you pause outside the house where he was born (there is nothing related to him to see inside, nor is the interior accessible to non-residents), by contrast, you can ponder the grim circumstances under which he lived out his first years. This is a side of his life most Swedes will be unaware of.

He was born on 28 May 1853, and his parents ran an inn which did not serve alcohol. Such a business, an inn for the sober, was doomed, and ended in bankruptcy. After the inn failed, his father abandoned the family, and Carl and his mother ended up on the street, destitute. One of the strongest memories the boy had of his father was when he told his son that he cursed the day his offspring had been born.

Social conditions in Old Town were generally quite deplorable at that time, and Carl Larsson's rise to national fame and fortune is a classic rags-to-riches story. Young Carl was convinced from early on that he was destined for greater things, and his memoirs describe his youthful self-image as 'a born knight among the riff-raff (*en boren riddare bland slöddret*). He remained haunted by his unhappy childhood and felt that his famously smiling and light-hearted persona was but a mask hiding his true self.

The plaque was mounted on the house in 1920 by Stockholms-Gillet (The Stockholm Guild), an organisation founded in 1914 that was considered controversial in later years (end of the 1980s) for its staunch refusal to allow women to become members (a policy that has now been revised).

The sculpted face of Carl Larsson in the plaque looks as firm and confident as always, in spite of the graffiti, but who knows what gloomy thoughts are hidden behind his ample moustache and little beard.

# BLACK FRIARS' CELLAR

*A hidden, atmospheric cellar*

*Södra Benickebrinken 4*
*Guided tours for groups can be booked through the Stockholm Medieval Museum:*
*medeltidsmuseet.stockholm/besok/historiska-rum/svartbrodraklostrets-kallare*
*Metro: Gamla stan*

© Fredriksson, Göran H.

**B**ehind a small, anonymous black iron door on Södra Benickebrinken 4 is the entrance to the preserved cellar of the Black Friars' monastery (the name Black Friars comes from the black cloaks the brothers of the Dominican order wore over their white habits). As you enter down a narrow flight of stairs to the dimly lit medieval brick arches, the cool cellar air grasps you with its ghostly fingers. The remnants of the past include a fireplace and the beautiful floor made in the 13th century from Gotland chalkstone.

The cellar probably functioned as a hostel for pilgrims that came to Stockholm because of a miraculous altarpiece (see below). Visiting today, it is easy to imagine how they huddled together among the subterranean archways, often ill or beset by life's troubles – and hoping desperately their journey to this city would set things right.

The atmospheric space now constitutes the only visible remains of a once extensive structure and very prominent monastic order. The monastery was the last of three to be founded in Stockholm, when King Magnus Eriksson donated land to the order in 1336.

## A miraculous silver image

The Black Friars had a steady income due to a special artefact in their possession: an altarpiece of gilded silver which attracted visitors from near and far and made the monastery and its church a pilgrimage site. Depicting Christ being taken down from the cross, the silver image was said to hold miraculous powers that those who gave donations could benefit from. Many such stories are recorded in a legendarium from the early 15th century. For example, a paralysed woman was cured, and a boy who drowned (and lay under the ice for several hours) was resurrected by it, as was a soldier shot through the neck with an arrow. When King Gustav Vasa of Sweden converted to Protestantism, he banished all Catholic holy orders from the land. The Dominican monastery was dissolved in 1528 and its buildings torn down. This took place over several years, with some structures left standing until 1547. The building material was carted away and used for the Royal Castle. King Gustav also took the altarpiece and melted it down – or had his chancellor pawn it in Bremen, Germany, according to one version. Its exact fate remains unknown and there has been speculation about it having been buried beneath the foundations of the order's property when they were banished. Extensive archaeological digs in moderns times have failed to turn anything up, but some remain convinced it is concealed beneath the cellar vaults.

# THE RELIEF OF HUSET BRASAN

*A mysterious relief of infernal or saintly significance*

*Kindstugatan 18*
*The house can be viewed from the outside at all times. The relief is in the*
*stairway and can be seen through the glass of the outer door*
*Metro: Gamla stan*

**A**t the corner of Kindstugatan and Svartmannagatan, Huset Brasan (The House of the Bonfire) gets its name from a mysterious relief, with a much-debated motif that used to be mounted on its facade, but now hangs in the stairwell of Kindstugatan 18.

The relief, bearing the date 1558 and the initials HQ, depicts a knight (or possibly simply a man in 16th-century clothing) and a monk. The figures, bound together at the neck, are blowing on a bonfire. In spite of it quite clearly showing two male, bearded figures, one interpretation of it has been that its motif shows a man and his wife who were unable to stop arguing and were therefore sentenced in 1558 to keep a fire burning together. A different interpretation says the figures are a baker and his wife hanged for producing sub-standard bread, but who were first forced to have a taste of the infernal torments awaiting them in the eternal fires of hell. A third theory states the relief was simply a

sign warning people of the dangers of fire in the narrow streets of Old Town.

Historians are generally of a different opinion altogether. According to them, the figures are St Cosmas and St Damian. They were twin brothers, both physicians, martyred in Syria in either the year 287 or 303. After their canonisation, they became the patron saints of surgeons. However, they are not usually depicted as a monk and a knight (though they were military doctors, so this might be an iconography reflecting this double nature of their work), nor are they connected to fire symbolism (they were executed by being hung on crosses, stoned, shot with arrows and, finally, beheaded). So, this interpretation does not seem clear-cut either.

More certain is that the initials HQ on the relief belonged to the Stockholm surgeon Henry Quant, who had it made and installed when he lived in the house during the middle of the 16th century. This, then, strengthens the case for the figures being (an atypical version of) the twin saints.

St Cosmas and St Damian were thought to offer protection against the plague, and in the 16th century (when the relief was made), Sweden was hit by more than a dozen outbreaks of plague. It may therefore have been the saints' supposed power to protect against this disease that partly motivated its creation.

# THE BURNT LOT

*A hidden oasis with a quiet atmosphere*

*Brända Tomten square (intersection of Kindstugatan and Själagårdsgatan)*
*Metro: Gamla stan*

Situated in a quiet part of Old Town, slightly off the most well-beaten tourist path, the tranquillity of the small square Brända Tomten (The Burnt Lot) is hard to match.

The name Brända Tomten first occurs in official records in 1760. Originally, a small house stood there, but it burnt down in 1728. The owner of the lot never put a new building in its place. Soon the horse and cart drivers discovered it was a useful spot to turn their equipages around, which was difficult in the narrow alleys of Old Town.

One of Sweden's most famous authors, August Strindberg (1849–1912), wrote a play toward the end of his life with the name *Brända Tomten* (1907), but it seems to refer to the subsequently demolished house close to Riddarholmen, where he was born. Nevertheless, the site in Old Town would certainly make a perfect place for staging Strindberg's highly symbolic chamber play.

Now, the primary function of the square is as a spot for contemplation, reading and picnics. Senior citizens, students and others come and go on the comfortable benches. Some take a thermos, and many sit there to read a book or newspaper. Being to some extent hidden away, it is seldom crowded. A few years ago, a cafe opened in one of the square's buildings, ever so slightly disrupting the quiet atmosphere. Many still choose to take their own coffee and snacks to eat in the shade of the great conker tree in the middle of the square.

## Beware!

In spite of being one of the most pleasant places in Stockholm to sit and rest, Brända Tomten also has a dangerous side in autumn. During September and October, the conker tree releases its spiky capsules onto the benches. One of these green balls landing on a head is enough to cause a nasty bump. Wear your medieval knight's helmet when reclining on the benches in autumn!

# THE ROSE DOOR

*Stockholm's oldest door and a pirate's insignia?*

Staffan sasses gränd, accessed from Köpmangatan
Metro: Gamla stan

At the end of the extremely short and easy-to-miss dead-end side street Staffan Sasses gränd (Staffan Sasse's Alley), the small rose-adorned door (dated around 1580) is often said to be Stockholm's oldest. As you pass through the low portal that constitutes the first part of the alley, you enter a tiny, atmospheric yard where memories of the past still seem strangely alive.

The alley is named after Staffan (or Stefan) Sasse (ca. 1500–1566), who was born in Lübeck, Germany, and served as a privateer captain in the service of the Swedish king Sten Sture the Younger (i.e., a sort of pirate who preyed on the ships of the enemies of Sweden). Under King Gustav Vasa's reign he became an admiral and held several important non-navy positions.

Sasse is known for having been one of the contestants in the tournaments, involving full knight's armour and sharp weapons, organised by Gustav Vasa when he married off the widows and daughters of the victims of the Stockholm Bloodbath (see p. 40). He did not fare well, perhaps being a better fighter on the deck of a ship than on horseback. Even so, he later got to marry Margareta Bengtsdotter of the noble Ulv family. In July 1524, the former pirate bought a house on Köpmannagatan. The narrow alley behind it accordingly ended up being called Staffan Sasse's Alley – a name mentioned in documents from 1569. Later it changed names several times, for example being called Ignatiigränd after the pioneering book publisher and printer Ignatius Meurer (1586–1672). In 1925 the name was changed back to its original one. The roses carved in stone around the door probably refer to the roses in Sasse's escutcheon (heraldic insignia).

There is a competing story about the rose-adorned door, which does not involve pirates, but is decidedly romantic in a different manner. According to that narrative, this was the house where Karin Månsdotter, then a maid in the Royal Castle, lived. In 1563, King Erik XIV fell madly in love with Karin and made her his mistress. She then gave birth to two sons. This was not unusual, but the king's subsequent decision to marry his mistress and make her queen certainly was. Not everyone was pleased with this elevation of a commoner, whose father was a prison warden, and it added to a brewing discontent with Erik XIV.

In one of the more well-known episodes of Swedish history, he was deposed and later murdered (according to tradition, he ate poisoned pea soup). Karin was, oddly, given a grand estate in Finland (then part of Sweden) by the new rulers, and became known for her kindness to the poor. She was buried in Åbo, Finland, and her grave is still regularly strewn with flowers by unknown admirers. Perhaps roses?

# DRAYMEN'S GUILD ROOMS

*The unique premises of the last active guild*

*Stora hoparegränd 6*
*Guided tours for groups can be booked through the Stockholm Medieval Museum:*
*medeltidsmuseet.stockholm/besok/historiska-rum/vindragarlagets-skralokal*
*Metro: Gamla stan*

The draymen (or wine carriers, in Swedish 'Vindragarlaget') were Sweden's last active guild, and in the building at Stora hoparegränd 6, their headquarters for the period 1818–1930 are preserved. In the gateway to the building, two of the tools of wine carriers – a special knife and an instrument used to extract wine – can be seen carved in stone.

The guild also maintained a hostel, the interior of which remains unchanged from how it looked in 1930, including the ancient furniture and various tools hanging on the walls. One particularly interesting object is the guild coffer, dated 1750. The premises are the only Swedish guild headquarters that have been preserved in their original condition in their original location.

Draymen were an important group in Stockholm, existing from the Middle Ages until 1930. As a profession whose services were crucial to taverns, restaurants and private homes in the city, a guild was organised in the 15th century (though a proper guild constitution was established only as late as 1686). The draymen were responsible for the transportation of barrels of wine from the harbour. They also handled the tapping and bottling of wine and spirits. When the alcohol arrived by ship, the draymen assisted the customs officers by opening the barrels and controlling the quality and alcohol content of the liquid within. Other imported liquids (e.g. syrup and some types of oil) were also the exclusive province of the Draymen's Guild. Finally, they had partial responsibility for firefighting and peacekeeping.

The number of draymen was limited to 17 – no more or less at any time – and this may be the origin of the Swedish expletive expression 'För 17 gubbar!' ('For the sake of 17 fellows!'). A drayman naturally had to be very strong, and wore a heavy leather apron for protection when handling the hefty barrels (which often had sharp studs or protruding splinters).

When mandatory membership of guilds was abolished in 1846, most guilds disappeared, but the draymen fought a protracted battle to preserve the existence and privileges of theirs. With labour unions being organised in the harbour, the draymen ended up in conflict with them. Eventually their relevance faded, and the last drayman retired in 1924 (though the guild was formally dissolved only in 1930). The state monopoly on alcohol sales made them completely redundant.

© Ek, Mattias

# ANCKARSTRÖM'S GUNS IN THE ROYAL ARMOURY

## *Haunted pistols from a regicide*

*Royal Armoury*
*Slottsbacken 3*
*Tuesday to Sunday 11am–5pm, Thursday 11am–8pm, closed Mondays*
*Entrance fee for adults, free on Thursdays*
*Metro: Gamla stan*

The dimly lit vaults of the Royal Armoury hold many noteworthy objects, including items relating to the spectacular death of one of the country's most famous kings: Gustav III. It houses the masquerade costume and bullet-pierced, bloodied undershirt he wore when he was assassinated at the Royal Swedish Opera in March 1792. Alongside them lie the guns and ammunition used to accomplish the dark deed.

There were several assassins and conspirators, but Captain Jacob Johan Anckarström (1762–1792) was the only one executed for his participation.

Gustav III had become unpopular with the nobility and army officers after a coup and reforms that increased the king's power, coupled with failed wars against neighbouring countries.

Anckarström was a nobleman and an officer who, with a general and several others, decided regicide was the only solution to the perceived national crisis. A group of them therefore shot the king, who died from blood poisoning two weeks later. The day after the shooting, Anckarström was apprehended, with the two pistols found at the crime scene leading investigators to him. A month after the king's death, Anckarström was publicly flogged on three consecutive days and then decapitated.

Weapons used to kill a king are charged with a special aura to many people. Accordingly, there are stories of Anckarström's pistols dancing around wildly at night in their display case and frightening the night guard witless. This purportedly happened several times in the old premises of the Royal Armoury, but the pistols are supposed to have rested still after the move to the present location.

## Alchemical ammunition?

In his entertaining novel *Alkemistens dotter* (*The Alchemist's Daughter*, 2014), alchemy expert Dr C.M. Edenborg portrays Anckarström as belonging to a clan of rebels that shot Gustav III with a mix of lead and iron, in accordance with alchemical operations in which those two metals 'kill the gold' – the gold here being the king. It is true that Anckarström came from a family background in alchemy, as his father was fanatical about such pursuits and had an advanced alchemical laboratory constantly in operation at the family estate.

# OLD PUBLIC URINAL

*The sexual secrets of King Gustav V*

*Next to Storkyrkan*
*Metro: Gamla stan*

The modern public urinal, or *pissoar* as it is called in vernacular Swedish, is a French invention, and was first seen on Paris boulevards in 1830. It did, however, have predecessors already in the Roman Empire. The idea, of course, is to keep men from urinating on the walls of houses, in stairways and parks, and so on. The first French versions were cylindrical one-man affairs, but they were eventually (in the 1870s) replaced in their native country by a multi-compartment variety. In the 1860s, the invention had spread to Berlin and, subsequently, reached cities further north, like Stockholm.

The earliest dated usage of the word in Swedish seems to go back to 1868, but the rather vulgar word *pissa* (take a piss) was in use at least as early as 1541. It seems to be derived from the Old French *pissier* (modern French: *pisser*), but may have entered Swedish via similar words in German, Dutch or some other language. One early example of its use is found in a record of a man excommunicated for urinating in church during Easter. Urinating in or on churches was equally frowned upon a few hundred years later, and in Old Town we can thus find a lavishly decorated pissoar strategically close to Storkyrkan, the oldest church in the area. Back in the day, the whole city was full of them. Installed in 1890, it is probably the only 19th-century model surviving today.

The hotspot for male prostitution during the late 19th century seems to have been now posh Östermalm, where most of the army barracks were located. Soldiers were highly masculine in their uniforms, clean, physically fit and, moreover, deloused – making them attractive to wealthy, older gay men on the prowl. The soldiers were often far away from home, in need of money, and sometimes also with emotional needs that could be fulfilled during encounters that involved both intimacy and an economic transaction. Urinals, for example the one on Nybroplan, were known meeting points, so police watched them closely.

Given the presence of quite a few soldiers guarding the Royal Castle, a short stroll across the square from the Old Town urinal, it is not entirely far-fetched to imagine similar things going on there as well. Persistent rumours have it that King Gustav V (1858–1950) was a closet homosexual. He succeeded his father, Oscar II, in 1907, and some fanciful historians of gay culture have suggested Prince Gustav was pleased the urinals were close to the castle, offering incognito gay cruising.

# IRON BOY SCULPTURE

*Sweden's (perhaps) smallest sculpture, said to have supernatural, wish-granting powers*

*Bollhustäppan, by Finska kyrkan, opposite the Royal Castle*
*Metro: Gamla stan*

Järnpojken (the iron boy) – in Bollhustäppan, a peaceful square tucked away behind the Finnish church right opposite the Royal Castle in Old Town, but unknown to most people – has been called Sweden's smallest sculpture.

This may or may not be correct.

Officially called *Pojke som tittar på månen* (*Boy looking at the moon*), the sculpture was made by Liss Eriksson (1919–2000) and inaugurated in 1967. It portrays a small boy looking towards the sky.

In the late 1980s, someone – perhaps an Old Town resident – dressed the boy in a woollen cap and a matching scarf. Local newspapers provided delighted reports on this precursor to the urban knitting phenomenon. On Midsummer Eve, the boy was provided with a tiny flower wreath, which is traditionally worn during these celebrations in Sweden. The small statue, now nicknamed Olle, soon became the subject of an odd spontaneous custom: passers-by started to offer him small coins, and were supposed to stroke their foreheads while mumbling a wish he supposedly had the power to grant. Stealing money from the little figure came to be considered severely unlucky. The custom of gifts and making wishes continues to this day.

Bollhustäppan is, unlike most other things in Old Town, not very old itself, and it was occupied by a house until the 1960s. When it was demolished, this hidden little square was created. It was restored in 2002 and became better lit at this point. Earlier, it had been something of a hangout for shady characters.

---

Liss Eriksson produced many sculptures during his career, but they tend to be on the monumental rather than the minuscule side of the scale (see, for example, his huge granite hands, *La Mano*, on Katarinavägen, close to Slussen). He often sculpted decorations for churches, and perhaps something of this sacred atmosphere carried over in his work on little Olle, prompting people to believe the figure has supernatural, wish-granting powers.

---

## The site of the first theatre with plays in Swedish

In the early 18th century, Bollhustäppan was the site of the first theatre offering plays in Swedish (most plays had previously been performed in French, the language of the cultured elite).

# 92 BLOODBATH STONES

(14)

*White stones supposedly commemorating those executed in the Stockholm Bloodbath of 1520*

*Schantzska huset, Stortorget 18*
*Metro: Gamla stan*

In local lore, the so-called Schantz house (erected, or at least heavily modified from an existing building, around 1650) on Stortorget 18 has been linked to the Stockholm Bloodbath of 1520 (see following double page).

Facing the square where the executions took place, it is often said that the 92 decorative white stones dotting the front of the building are meant to commemorate the victims. The man responsible for the stones would have been the house's owner, Johan Eberhard Schantz, who was the secretary of King Karl X.

One story has it that as long as the stones remain in place, the spirits of the dead are at peace, perhaps because of being commemorated in this way. Should the stones be displaced, though, ghosts would haunt the streets in anger.

In fact, there seems to be little historical basis for the stones being intended to represent the bloodbath victims. And if you count the stones carefully, there are 94 of them (it should be said, on the other hand, that there are different opinions on how many died on the fateful November days in 1520).

The building was merged from Stortorget 18–20 in the 17th century, and it was Schantz who then added grand details like the portal flanked by reclining Roman warriors. Above the portal is also an inscription in German from Psalm 37:5: 'Befiehl dem Herrn deine Wege und hoffe auf ihn, er wirds wohl machen' (Commit thy way unto the Lord; trust also in him; and he shall bring it to pass).

© Richard Mortel, via Wikimedia Commons

## The Stockholm Bloodbath of 1520

A national trauma with long-lasting effects, the so-called Stockholm Bloodbath of 1520 not only changed the course of Swedish history but also became a motif in folklore and popular fiction. On 9 and 10 November that year, around 92 people (sources differ) were executed by hanging or decapitation in Stortorget (the Great Square) in Old Town. Somewhat similar to the infamous 'Red Wedding' in *Game of Thrones*, events started with the Danish King Christian II inviting the Swedish nobility to the Royal Castle in Stockholm to celebrate his coronation as king not only of Denmark, but also of Sweden.

The latter country had attained independence from Denmark through the efforts of the Sture family, but the Sture army was defeated by Christian II in September 1520. Subsequently, in a seemingly generous gesture, he pardoned all his former enemies among the high-ranking families. This having been formalised in an official document, he was given the keys to Stockholm by the mayor and entered the city in grand style.

One of his allies was the Swedish Archbishop Gustavus Trolle (at this point recently reappointed by Christian II to this office, which the Sture regent had removed him from). The archbishop now sensed an opportunity to use the new situation to get back at some of his enemies from earlier internal power struggles. Many of these were conveniently also part of the Sture alliance, so Christian II would have been easy to convince they needed to be disposed of. Hence, in the twilight hours of November 8, Danish soldiers brandishing torches and lanterns entered the great hall of the Royal Castle and apprehended those of the guests that were on a list made by Trolle. Over the following two days, they were executed (together with a number of commoners) and, according to several accounts, the streets of Old Town literally ran red with blood.

The idea of making an example of the victims of this massacre, and thus securing the Danish grip on Sweden, decidedly misfired. Instead, the son of one of those executed instigated a full-scale rebellion against the Danes and was later crowned King Gustav Vasa of Sweden. Never again would Sweden be under foreign rule, and the relation to Denmark remained frosty for centuries. King Christian II is known in Sweden as Christian the Tyrant, while a well-known – but totally inaccurate – story claims the Danes designated him Christian the Good.

There are many tales of the ghosts of King Christian's victims haunting Old Town, and on 9–10 November the cobblestones supposedly turn red.

© Michael Sittow, Public domain, via Wikimedia Commons

# CANNONBALL IN THE WALL

*A historical relic that is a by-product of a king's
fanatical interest in stage art*

*Corner of Stortorget and Skomakargatan
Metro: Gamla stan*

I f you look up when standing on the corner of Stortorget and Sko-makargatan, you see a cannonball protruding from the wall above. According to legend, it was fired in the first year of the on-and-off 1521–1523 siege when Stockholm was liberated from the yoke of the (in the opinion of many Swedes) nefarious Danish King Christian the Tyrant. Supposedly, it was aimed at the crowned Danish head but narrowly missed its target and ended up stuck there.

The story about 'the ball in the wall' having ended up there in 1521, though entertaining, is unfortunately not true.

It was put there by the wealthy furniture dealer Fredrik Christian Hans Grevesmuhl in 1795, when he had the house built. His intention with this unusual decoration seems to have been to make reference to the military victory of Gustav Vasa (subsequently the king of Sweden) over King Christian (a feat based on perseverance and tough negotiations, rather than any dramatic, decisive battle on the walls of the city), for it to serve as a nationalistic celebration of Swedish independence.

It is thus not completely unconnected to the events of 1521, but says more about Swedish pride over them in a later period.

This attitude was encouraged in particular by King Gustav III (1746–1792), the so-called 'theatre king'. Gustav III was not only enthusiastic about watching different types of stage productions, but also enjoyed directing, writing and performing in them. He began his career as a playwright in childhood, with several French-language pieces. Together with Johan Henric Kellgren (1751–1795), he wrote the libretto for the 1786 opera *Gustaf Wasa* by Johann Gottlieb Naumann (1741–1801; ironically, Naumann, who was German, also worked for the Danish court and composed operas in Denmark). One of the central parts of the narrative in this opera is the siege of Stockholm. It became wildly popular and was performed 177 times between 1786 and 1886. The aria *Ädla skuggor, vördade fäder* (*Noble shadows, revered fathers*) became a sort of early equivalent of a national anthem.

It was probably this opera which, towards the end of the 18th century, renewed interest in the siege as a source of great national pride. This, then, is the context in which the inventive 1795 house decoration by the furniture dealer must be seen.

# THE RUNE STONE CORNER

*A rune stone used as building material*

*Corner of Prästgatan and Kåkbrinken*
*Metro: Gamla stan*

Rune stones have not always been considered valuable relics. Medieval Swedes were seemingly unimpressed by the work of their pagan ancestors and even used rune stones as building material. The portion of such a stone incorporated in the outer wall of a house on the corner of Prästgatan and Kåkbrinken testifies as much.

It is one of three rune stones found in Old Town, but today is the only one that remains in the same location where it was first discovered by modern scholars (the other three have been removed from Old Town – two disappeared, and one is now in the Medieval Museum).

Analysis of the stone has shown that it was carved around 1000 CE, a couple of hundred years before the founding of Stockholm. The dating is based on, among other things, the fact that Frögunn – mentioned on the stone – is a distinctly pagan, rather than Christian name.

Where it was originally raised is not known, and it seems likely it was taken from somewhere else, possibly quite a distance away, to be used as building material. This was at a time when antiquarian interest in rune stones was still unheard of, and they were attractive simply as large, solid pieces of stone.

The text on it reads 'Torsten and Frögunn erected the stone in memory of their son'. Very few Stockholmers today would be able to read the inscription. The most likely competent readers would be the occasional person well-versed in ancient Norse lore and alphabets due to academic study, or the overlapping category of fantasy geeks who frequent the nearby Science Fiction-bokhandeln (The Science Fiction Bookshop – for decades Stockholm's main provider of fantastic literature).

Next to the rune stone is the barrel of a cannon, used to strengthen the corner of the wall. It would have been added in the 17th century, when heavier carts and carriages had started to be used on the narrow and often slippery streets of Old Town. This development caused the corners of many houses to be damaged, and various forms of protective supports were therefore added. Exactly in what context discarded cannon barrels became available to enterprising house owners is not clear. In older times, builders clearly had to make do with whatever material was at hand.

# FIRST-GENERATION
# PHONE BOOTH

*One of only three remaining booths in central Stockholm*

Next to Storkyrkan
Metro: Gamla stan

Once, phone booths were everywhere in Swedish cities. In the 1980s, there were 44,000 of them, but already by 2010 there were only 2,700. The ones still to be found today remain purely for their aesthetic and historical value. This means the phone booths most older Swedes once used frequently – the robust models from the 1970s and 80s – have vanished. The picturesque, turn-of-the-century type survive, and one of the prettiest is in Old Town. It is one of only three remaining booths in central Stockholm (the other two are at Kornhamnstorg and Mosebacke torg).

Of course, the reason for their disappearance is the arrival of mobiles phones. After it was announced in 2013 that the remaining booths would be sold to anyone interested, with prices ranging from a mere 1,500 to 3,000 Swedish crowns, it was only a matter of hours before all of them had changed hands. Presumably, most ended up as eccentric decorations in private houses and gardens. In 2015, the last booths were dismantled, except for the three highly decorative old-timey ones in Stockholm.

The first phone booth in Sweden was installed in Stockholm in the 1890s, or in 1901 according to some sources. This model, of which the one in Old Town is an example, was called 'the pagoda', for reasons that are obvious when you look at its shape. It was designed by the engineer Hjalmar Celion, who came up with a wide array of clever, functional features. To shut out distracting street noise, the walls were made from a soundproofing material and oak. The etched-glass windows were intended to make it easy to determine if the booth was in use by someone else. The grid at the bottom was supposed to protect the caller against dogs (!), though it remains a mystery if the problem with aggressive strays was big enough in Sweden to necessitate this. Equally obscure is *how* the grid would offer protection, as it does not cover the front of booth.

Around the turn of the century, the use of coins instead of special tokens started. This led to big problems with people attempting to steal the coins, and remained an issue until the phone card was introduced toward the end of the phone booth era. Such cards, which had all sorts of imaginative decorations, were for a while collector's items, but have, it seems, somewhat paradoxically decreased in popularity after they stopped being produced.

# HUSET KRONAN

*A remembrance of the day that things almost went very wrong*

*Storkyrkobrinken 3*
*Metro: Gamla stan*

Above the door on Storkyrkobrinken 3, a large gilded royal crown adorns the facade. A legend, documented in writing for more than 100 years (but it may be significantly older), records that it commemorates a fateful event on the coronation day of King Karl XII (1682–1718).

Famously a strong-willed and self-sufficient young man, King Karl XII has gone down in history as the only Swedish monarch to have put the crown on his own head during the coronation ceremony in Storkyrkan, taking it from the hands of the archbishop who should have placed it there. On his way from the church, the crown fell from his head. Had it landed on the ground, it would have been an ill omen indeed.

Of course, the king eventually came to a bad end, being shot in the head at the siege of Fredriksten. Before that, he achieved a number of impressive military victories, became the first king to allow Muslims to celebrate religious rites in Sweden and possibly played a key part in the importing of Turkish culinary culture.

Luckily, the crown that fell from his head was caught by count Johan Gabriel Stenbock (a relative of whom in the 19th century became a Gothic–Decadent author of strange tales of vampires and werewolves, and a friend of Oscar Wilde). This event is said to have taken place outside the house on Storkyrkobrinken 3, making the owner of the building commission a crown made from gilded sheet metal in remembrance of the day that things almost went very wrong.

The explanation is in all probability more prosaic. In the 19th century, the apothecaries of Stockholm were typically named after animals (see p. 136 on the owl apothecary) and would have a sculpture of its namesake above the door. Some also had other names, and thus a different sculpted decoration. This is one likely origin of the crown above the door.

Earlier theories have suggested it was a business sign for a goldsmith or a symbol of the royal post office, which used the building for a time. From 1756, for an unknown number of years, it seems to have been the site of one of Stockholm's early coffeehouses, but the crown is probably not related to this.

# THE PETRIFIED CAT BAS-RELIEF ⑲

*The colourful legend of the man-slaying talking cat and the poor sailor*

*Västerlånggatan 24*
*Metro: Gamla stan*

According to local folklore, the stone animal above the gate of Västerlånggatan 24 is a petrified cat. This is not actually the case, however, as scholars have demonstrated that it is not a cat but a marten, showing that a merchant dealing in animal skins had his business there.

The legend, as so often, is a lot more interesting than the truth. According to the most well-known tale, published in 1882, a sailor was rescued in a storm at sea by a water nymph. She made him promise that in return he would go to Västerlånggatan 24 immediately upon his arrival in Stockholm to deliver a letter to someone called Måns. The sailor postponed the task, and when he got there the only creature by that name turned out to be the house cat. To his surprise, the feline spoke to him in a human voice and, while reading the letter, became furious about the delay. The enraged cat slayed the sailor with his tiny claws, then jumped out the window, but stopped on the ledge above the door and turned to stone. The letter, left behind by the cat, was unreadable to everyone, since it was written in a strange, incomprehensible language.

The tale is one of many in a massive 600-page book, *Gamla Stockholm: Anteckningar ur tryckta och otryckta källor* (*Old Stockholm: Notes From Published and Unpublished Sources*). It was compiled by the young, radical author August Strindberg (1849–1912) and an older newspaper man, Claës Lundin (1825–1908). The latter also wrote the first Swedish science fiction novel, *Oxygen and Aromasia* (1878), which portrays Stockholm in the year 2378. Strindberg and Lundin did not get along, among other things, because the younger man felt his colleague was too slow and meticulous. There is good reason to assume the pair added to many of the popular, vernacular narratives in the book, filling in blanks, clarifying details and so on. The tale of the cat may therefore partly be a literary invention on their part. Nevertheless, if it was not established exactly in this form in local folklore (it may have been), it became so after the book's publication.

# GÅSGRÄND

*The lowest street in Stockholm*

*Metro: Gamla stan*

There are several ghost stories about a basement on Gåsgränd, a quaint street that ends in a short tunnel with a low ceiling (making it the lowest portion of any street in Stockholm with its 1.88-metre height).

The name means Geese Lane and is derived from a woman named Ragnhild Grågås (a surname meaning 'grey goose' in English). She died around 1510 and is recorded to have been accused, but acquitted, of having sex with the same man her daughter was also involved with. This was considered a serious crime and carried the death penalty. Ragnhild lived on this block, possibly on Gåsgränd itself. It is unclear why it was named after her.

## A haunted basement

Right after the tunnel portion of the street, there is a small square, created in the late 1770s as a space to turn carriages around. This is where the restaurant Gåsgränd 4 is located, with medieval underground vaults (the street-level house was built as late as 1837). In these vaults, inexplicable events are said to have taken place. A carpenter working on renovations there a few years ago claimed his tools kept disappearing and, having left a room for a mere 10 seconds, he came back to discover his planks of wood raised up with one of them balanced on top of the others. He was alone in the basement and the door above the stairs was locked. Also, the carpenter said the place was unnaturally cold and he had a frightening sensation of being watched.

A waitress at the restaurant has told of a disturbing occurrence as she was cleaning up one night: an invisible hand seemingly pulled at her trousers. This happened again on a later occasion when she was heading up from the vaults, almost making her fall on the dangerously steep stairs.

You can visit the basement during the opening hours of the restaurant (Sunday to Thursday 12–10pm, Friday to Saturday 12–11pm), though it seems the paranormal phenomena are limited to times when someone is alone.

The incidents above are reported on the blog of journalist and author Petter Inedahl and are both quite recent. The basement may be from the days of Ragnhild Grågås, and indeed some more historically specific ghost stories weave her into the narrative, claiming she takes orders for food from guests, who don't notice she is a phantom. When they ask the real staff what happened to their order, they are of course told that no order has been made.

# HELL ALLEY

*The darkest of dead ends*

*Northernmost part of Prästgatan*
*Metro: Gamla stan*

The short section of Prästgatan (Priest Street) that continues north of Tyska Brinken and ends in a dead end once had a more ominous name: Helvetesgränd (Hell Alley).

It seems to have been known under this name from at least 1529 (though there are mentions already in 1451 of a plot of land situated in 'hell') until 1885. It is easy enough to understand why the name was changed in 1885, but where did it come from?

This has been a matter of considerable and long-lasting academic dispute. A once popular theory had it that the name derived from the French philosopher Claude Adrien Helvétius (1715–1771), but the name is, as mentioned, documented long before this gentleman was born.

A more likely interpretation takes as its starting point the fact that in medieval Sweden, Helvetet ('Hell') was not uncommon as a name for farms, streets or parts of cities situated north of the local church. This reflects a notion of hell being located in the far north, rather than indicating that the places in question were particularly hellish or somehow connected to the powers of darkness. Even so, it certainly does not have a very pleasant ring to contemporary ears but may have been considered more neutral by medieval Swedes. To them, perhaps, it may simply have meant something 'to the north'.

A third interpretation links the name to a tradition saying Helvetesgränd was where Stockholm's executioner and torturer lived (in lodgings provided by the city). The central location would be a deterrent to the citizens, who could observe the executioner daily. He was a much-feared figure, and it was common for him to have a criminal background. Becoming an executioner could even be meted out as a punishment for crimes or be offered as an alternative to someone sentenced to death. The person would then have both ears cut off and be branded with the seal of the city. This prevented him from attempting to escape his gruesome tasks and the social ostracising they entailed. Executioners were generally hated, and even more so on the European continent, where they more often – compared with their colleagues in Sweden – had to torture prisoners and mete out capital punishments using particularly sadistic methods. This, perhaps, is why Stockholm executioners were on several occasions attacked by visiting foreigners. One of them was stoned so severely by German sailors that he could no longer work.

There are stories saying the ghost of at least one executioner still haunts this alley.

# CROSSED-OUT PLOMMENFELT FAMILY CREST

*The memory of a masonic necromancer*

*The House of Nobility*
*Riddarhustorget 10*
*Monday to Friday 11am–noon*
*Entrance fee*

The House of Nobility (*Riddarhuset*, literally 'the house of knights') is where Swedish nobles congregate for a variety of social events, and it also holds archives about this social class. For one hour per day, during the week, it is open to visitors. The highlight is the knights' hall, which was originally (1668–1865) used for the meetings of the nobility in the days when the Swedish parliament (*riksdag*) was drawn from the four estates: nobility, clergy, burghers and peasants. Every third year, a meeting of the nobility is still convened there and every noble family may send one male representative to attend (Swedish gender egalitarianism has not penetrated this institution yet). The walls of the knights' hall are covered with the crests of around 2,330 noble families, of which only around 700 remain in existence (i.e., have living descendants still bearing the name).

Intriguingly, one family crest to the immediate right of the entrance is crossed out with black lines. It belongs to the Plommenfelt family, which was stricken from the list of Swedish nobility (see following double page).

CARL ANDERS PLOMMENFELT
Silhuett

## *The scratch with the diamond ring*

A prominent freemason and a good friend of King Gustav III's younger brother duke Karl (later King Karl XIII), Carl Anders von Plommenfelt (1750–ca. 1785) was the member of the Plommenfelt family who caused them to be stricken from the list of Swedish nobility in 1782.

Rumour among his masonic brothers had it that Plommenfelt had the power to curse his enemies with illness and misfortune. He was also a driving force behind the experiments with communicating with spirits that Duke Karl participated in. Even the king himself took part in such necromantic rituals with Plommenfelt, and one documented instance – involving magic books, circles drawn with charcoal, mirrors, and ritual use of blood – allegedly resulted in spirits communicating with the magicians via rappings on the walls. However, he was not just a mystic but also a rather flawed human being who had lost his position as master of ceremonies at the Royal Castle after getting involved in a judicial process where he conducted himself badly.

Thus, on 17 March 1782, he was drowning his sorrows and (rather too loudly) lamenting his misfortune at the inn Clas på Hörnet (still in operation on Surbrunnsgatan 20). One of the windows was decorated with a portrait of Gustav III, beneath which was written (in French, the language preferred by the highest echelons of Swedish society at this time) 'the foremost citizen'. The bitter and drunken Plommenfelt caught sight of this and used his diamond ring to scratch an addendum to this on the window: 'he has been that but is now the foremost fool'. Later that day, a Major Lindestam noticed this outrageous scratching. He interrogated the staff and found out who the perpetrator of the lèse-majesté was, then set off to report him to the police. The innkeeper had the window removed.

The day after, two of Plommenfelt's masonic brothers – Adolf Fredrik Munck and Baron Gustaf Adolf Reuterholm – were informed of the event by the innkeeper and took away the window to protect their brother. When they learned Major Lindestam had already reported the crime, they realised their attempted cover-up might backfire on them, so they handed the window over to the king. Plommenfelt, having fled the country, was sentenced in his absence to death by decapitation and never set foot on Swedish soil again. Apparently, Plommenfelt's supposed esoteric powers did him no good at this time, and he died destitute, probably in America.

# SLIDES OF THE OLD NATIONAL ARCHIVE

## *The fireproof architecture of a sleeping beauty*

*Gamla riksarkivet*
*Arkivgatan 3, Riddarholmen*
*Open during events (at Yuletide, for instance, traditional Christmas lunch or dinner is given) or by being very charming*
*Metro: Gamla stan*

During World War II, it was feared that Stockholm might get invaded or bombed by the Germans. As a safety measure, special helter-skelter style spiral slides were therefore added to the National Archive building. Using this beautiful contraption, the bound volumes and bundles of documents could be swiftly gotten out of harm's way should the need arise. Needless to say, it never did. The slides still look amazing as a form of sculpture with a fascinating back story.

More or less an architectural sleeping beauty for almost 50 years, the old National Archive (Gamla riksarkivet) is one of few in Europe containing a well-preserved interior from the days it served as an institution of this type. In 1968, the National Archive moved to a new, and aesthetically quite unappealing, building. This left its old premises in a long-lasting limbo.

The old archive was built between 1887 and 1890, and was joined up with an adjacent structure, the Stenbock palace, where the archives had previously been kept.

To protect the obviously flammable collections of documents, the archive was given a cast-iron frame to minimise the wood elements. Even the bookcases were made of iron, and many of the doors were cut from the same type of sheet metal used for steamboat chimneys.

In spite of almost everything being made of metal and stone, the interior of the house has a surprisingly slender and light feel to it, which defies the weighty materials used. Fear of fire further led to the house not being provided with electricity (which was then, as now, a not uncommon source of house fires), and using candles was of course out of the question. To provide light, the house was therefore given oversized windows, by which the staff had to carry out their work.

Steam trains passing close to the house however ruined this plan somewhat, since the windows became covered in soot. Things grew even more problematic when the workday of the clerks was extended to six hours, making it difficult in the darkness of Nordic winters to actually labour throughout the entire day. At this point, electricity was installed. This also led to the house getting Sweden's first electrical elevator.

Today the building is in the hands of Stureplansgruppen, who lease it out for conferences, concerts and all sorts of other things. If the on-site staff are in a good mood, they will let you have a quick look around.

# MEDUSA HEAD
# IN RIDDARHOLMSKYRKAN

*Why is a Medusa head in a church?*

*Riddarhustorget, Riddarholmen*
*Daily mid-May to mid-September 10am-5pm*
*Saturday and Sunday mid-September to mid-November 10am–4pm*
*Entrance fee*
*Metro: Gamla stan*

When you enter Riddarholmskyrkan (The Knight's Church), a grotesquely beautiful Medusa's head, crowned with slithering serpents, greets you in a cavity close to the entrance. Lit in a way that makes it look even more nightmarish, it is a modern casting of a 17th-century facade decoration from the church. Why a Medusa head was chosen to decorate a church in the first place is unclear.

The cavity itself was a door in the 16th century, became a window in 1634, and was bricked up in 1651 when a new burial vault was built on the other side of the wall.

On display further in, on the right-hand side, is a plaster cast of the skull of King Karl Knutsson (ca. 1408/09–1470), made on the opening of his tomb in 1916. Such grim details add to the spooky atmosphere conjured up by the ghost stories surrounding the building (see below).

## A murder in a church

In 1382, Bo Jonsson Grip (ca. 1330–1386), the head of the Royal Council, broke the strict ban on violence in churches. Entering Riddarholmskyrkan, then still called the Greyfriars' Church (the cloister church of the Franciscan order in Stockholm), he attacked his relative, Carl Nilsson Färla, with his sword. The latter had had an affair with Grip's wife, and paid the price as he fell to the enraged husband's sword. In his fury, Grip is supposed to have hacked Färla's body to bits in front of the altar. The dismembered body was then buried in the church. According to an old story, the stone covering the grave subsequently cracked in as many pieces as the body had been cut into (the stone is no longer in place, unfortunately).

## Ghostly knocks of Colonel Gustavsson, the son of King Gustav III?

King Gustav III's son, Gustav IV Adolf, was an unpopular monarch. After being blamed for the events that led to the loss of the Swedish provinces in Finland to Russia, he was deposed of in a coup in early 1809. He then spent the rest of his life travelling through Europe under the assumed name Colonel Gustavsson (Gustav's son). Since 1634, Riddarholmskyrkan had served as the burial site of Swedish royalty. When Gustav IV Adolf died in Switzerland on 7 February 1837, his remains were not taken back to the church in Sweden immediately (in fact, they were interred there only 47 years later).

A ghostly tale states that at midnight on the day after his death, the guardian at Riddarholmskyrkan heard three hard knocks on the door of the building. No one was outside when the door was opened. Supposedly, this was the unhappy spirit of Colonel Gustavsson wanting to enter what should have been his natural place of burial.

# Södermalm

1. SKANSTULL CHOLERA GRAVEYARD — 68
2. JULIUS HUS — 70
3. KATARINA FIRE STATION'S LANTERN — 72
4. THE DECORATION OF THE COPPER DOORS OF ÖSTGÖTAGATAN 14 — 74
5. THE CRACKS OF THE BELL OF KATARINA CHURCH — 76
6. ERSTA COMMUNION WAFER BAKERY — 78
7. TEATER DUR OCH MOLL — 80

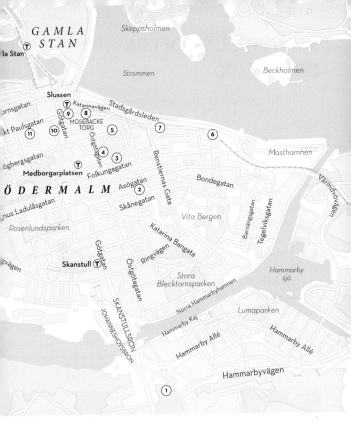

⑧ CAPTAIN ROLLA MONUMENT — 82

⑨ THE BELLMAN HOUSE — 84

⑩ THE ALMGREN FACTORY — 88

⑪ MERMAID STATUES AT THE VAN DER NOOT PALACE — 92

⑫ JAS 39 GRIPEN CRASH MEMORIAL — 94

⑬ MINIATURE REPLICA OF MICKES SERIER, CD & VINYL — 96

⑭ REIMERSHOLME VODKA BENCHES — 98

# SKANSTULL CHOLERA GRAVEYARD

*A ghostly pandemic burial ground*

*Skansbacken 6*
*Open 24/7*
*Metro: Gullmarsplan*

Fancy a walk among the graves of pandemic victims? In the Skanstull graveyard for the victims of the 1834 and 1853 cholera outbreaks in Stockholm, it's slightly more pleasant than it might sound. The adjacent motorway is today probably the most unpleasant aspect.

Opened in 1809, it was originally created primarily for the soldiers who died in the war with Russia and Denmark (many of them succumbing to various illnesses rather than enemy bullets or sabres). It was also used for unidentified corpses found in the city and those who died while in police custody. These graves were located in the south-east part of the present-day graveyard.

Local authorities in the 1830s knew well in advance that cholera was approaching from the continent and designated this graveyard for the inevitable. When cholera hit, it hit hard. Almost four thousand people died at a rate of 120 a day, and horse-drawn carriages transported piles

© Kolerakyrkogården, Skanstull

of bodies to the graveyard every night. As many as 16 coffins were put in each of the deeply dug graves. A second cholera outbreak occurred in 1853, this time taking almost three thousand lives, with corpse carriages running in shuttle traffic once more. Cholera returned almost yearly until 1894, though never again quite so severely.

By the 1850s, a connection to lacking hygiene was suspected, and mainly because of this the city assumed responsibility for emptying Stockholm's latrines in 1859.

The creation of a municipal water treatment plant in 1861 drastically reduced the number of deaths in the following outbreaks. In 1884, the role of bad hygiene in the spread of cholera was scientifically proved, and a decade later the disease was virtually non-existent in Stockholm. The cholera graveyard remained in use until 1901.

Among the most moving gravestones is the minimalistic marker bearing the simple carving 'Elin', with no dates or other information. There are also many children's graves, for 'Little Carl', 'Little David', and so on. Graves for adults often state the profession of the deceased, for example 'The fishmonger W. Lundgren'.

The red-painted 1832 gravedigger's cottage, which retains its original floor plan, offers an interesting glimpse of the period's living conditions. A widow named Anna Hedvig Nessen held the grim job for the first 15 years, after which she was succeeded by her two children.

© Jordgubbe

# JULIUS HUS

*The domain of a bread king of yore*

*Bondegatan 21A*
*Check website for events: juliushus.se*
*Courtyard open during normal office hours*
*Metro: Medborgarplatsen*

In the courtyard of the place where a small bakery empire started, Stockholm's entrepreneurial history remains vividly alive and the atmosphere of old Stockholm is tangible.

The entrance to the courtyard features interesting little displays of old bread labels and marketing posters, as well as informative films about the history of the founding family shown on a screen at the far end of the archway. The stairs on the right have an old, preserved sign saying 'kontor' (office) with a golden arrow pointing up.

Founder Julius Westerdahl (1846–1926) served as a field baker in the Russo–Turkish War of 1877–1878, and on his return to Stockholm became responsible for a small bakery on the corner of Åsögatan and Södermannagatan. During the war, he learnt the Russian way to make crispbread by leaving the dough out during snowfall – so-called cold fermentation (kalljäsning). This was the origin of his innovation *delikatessbröd* (delicacy bread), an extra-thin crispbread he prepared using ice during the fermentation. This new bread became a hit, and Westerdahl won multiple awards for it.

At first, he delivered the product himself with a wheelbarrow. In 1884, he became official supplier to the Royal Court and built a bigger, more modern bakery along with a representative house for himself and his family. In 1904 he added further buildings and, in 1924, stables.

Julius Westerdahl's son would go on running the flourishing bakery business. He also started retail franchises and went into the business of manufacturing surgical instruments and hygiene products. In 1941, bread company Wasa bought the bakery and the rights to delikatessbröd, which is still available in most food stores.

All the buildings Julius Westerdahl erected on Bondegatan remain and are today mostly the offices of various creative businesses.

## Rent Westerdahl's historical living quarters

The Westerdahl family lived in the building for five generations. Julius' great-granddaughter has renovated the opulent living quarters, which can be rented for conferences and events (and open quite regularly for public events like chamber music concerts or tea salons).

They feature a dining room with dark wooden panelling and a complex intarsia floor, a music room with a 1919 Steinway piano and several beautiful smaller rooms, all with antique furnishings.

# KATARINA FIRE STATION LANTERN

*The world's (probably) oldest operational fire station*

*Tjärhovsgatan 9–11*
*The lantern and garage can be viewed all day*

It seems likely that Katarina fire station is the oldest one that remains operational in its original location – the closest competitor being an American station running since 1889. A process to get this acknowledged in *Guinness World Records* has started. Yet, most of the interior that can be seen through the garage doors looks more functionally modern than quaintly archaic, a prioritisation which is only to be expected.

The oldest parts of the building date back to the 1870s. After having served as a brewery, city watch quarters, and an extra hospital during the 1834 cholera epidemic, it became a fire station in 1876. In 1895, major reconstructions were made, with several smaller buildings that were part of the complex being torn down and new ones replacing them. Nine horses pulled the fire carts at that time but were eventually replaced by cars. In 1914, the stables were turned into a garage. The last horses, Max and Dux, were sold off in 1916.

The final major makeover of the station was in the 1980s. Today, around 45 firemen work there, protecting a district of 120,000 people from the ravages of fire.

## NEARBY
### Firefighting museum
*The museum is only shown to groups of five to twenty visitors and must be prebooked (via Christer Lundell: 209ludde@gmail.com)*
*Entrance fee*
At the back of Katarina fire station (in another stable building) is a firefighting museum run by firemen volunteers since 1993. It features historical photographs, folk art with firefighting-related motifs, banners, old fire trucks and carriages, uniforms, hoses, gas masks and other equipment.

# THE DECORATION OF
# THE COPPER DOORS
# OF ÖSTGÖTAGATAN 14

*Peculiarly decorated transformer station doors*

*Östgötagatan 14*
*Metro: Medborgarplatsen*

On a back street leading down from Mosebacke, two gigantic pairs of mysterious copper doors reach several metres up. It looks almost as if an explosion has occurred on the other side, deforming them.

On closer inspection, the bumpy and craggy surface on the right pair of doors turns out to have various electrical appliances incorporated, like waffle irons and flat irons. The explanation is that behind them is a transformer station. And yes, an explosion – albeit a well-controlled one – did indeed create their distinctive surface.

Built between 1903 and 1905 to a design by Ferdinand Boberg, this transformer station performed the essential task of converting the electrical energy that arrived at several thousands of volts from the distribution grid into the low voltage required in the homes of Södermalm.

Boberg had been inspired by seeing Moorish–Islamic architecture during a trip to Morocco, and even went so far as to have the building face Mecca. It is therefore highly fitting that it became Stockholm's first major mosque. Since the year 2000, the entire building has been used as a mosque and Islamic cultural centre, and the prayer room is now located behind the tile walls of the former machine hall. The conversion into a mosque took place between 1996 and 2000, when a minaret was added.

The decorative copper doors toward Östgötagatan were installed when the building was expanded in 1992. The artist Mikael Pauli was hired to provide suitable decorations and decided to use welded copper plates shaped by a controlled explosion. An expert in explosives from the company Nitro Nobel was consulted. The doors were softened in an industrial oven and then dug into a pit in the ground. The waffle irons and other appliances were put on top of one pair of doors before the ex-

plosives were set off, and the other was decorated with bolts illustrating the movement of electrical energy within an electrical cord. There was only one shot at getting it right, but luckily everything turned out as hoped.

Behind the doors is a massive layer of concrete, to provide the necessary blast safety in case of an explosion in the transformer station. The fact that the doors have been shaped by a blast is an amusing nod to this. They are also a wonderfully tactile experience, so take the opportunity to touch them.

# THE CRACKS OF THE BELL OF KATARINA CHURCH

## *A fire-damaged bell*

*Högbergsgatan 15*
*Metro: Slussen*

Outside Katarina Church, a huge, damaged church bell – with a prominent crack along one side – rests on the ground. The bell was damaged in a 1990 fire, after which it was placed there as a remembrance of the grim might of combustion.

This was not the first time the beautiful baroque Katarina Church burnt. It was badly damaged in a fire in 1723, when the bells melted and the liquid dripped down into the church below. When it was rebuilt, the cupola became higher and more impressive.

# Katarina Church and the history of witchcraft in Sweden

Katarina Church is closely tied to the history of witchcraft in Sweden. In the late 17th century (starting in 1670), special prayers for protection against witches were read there. At the time, dramatic witch trials were being held in several places in Sweden. The fear of Satan's servants reached a pitch in Stockholm in 1675 when a young boy arrived from Gävle, where his mother had been executed for witchcraft. He soon started making bizarre allegations about his neighbours and was joined by others equally eager to denounce people as Satanists. Most of the accusers and the supposed witches all lived within a few blocks of Katarina Church. In a room above the sacristy of the church, a consortium investigating the charges against suspected witches convened. In total, eight women were executed. One of them was burnt alive since she had refused to confess to being a witch. Eventually, the informers were more closely scrutinised, and it turned out they had made the whole thing up. The women still held in custody were released and the informants executed in their stead. The ashes of the most fervent informer, Lisbeth Carlsdotter, still rest somewhere in the cemetery surrounding Katarina Church. In 1779 the capital punishment for sorcery was abolished in Sweden, but occasional outbreaks of rumour and panic still occurred much later – often with tragic consequences. Because of Katarina Church's historical connections to the witch trials, it has been suggested that the two fires of 1723 and 1990 were retribution for the cruelties of the church toward the witches. Some say the fires are a 'divine retribution' of sorts, with God avenging himself on his inhumane and intolerant earthly servants. Others claim the church was cursed by the witches. Local lore even has it that a secretive witch cult, existent throughout the centuries, was behind the fires as payback for their executed members. An alternative supernatural explanation for the misfortunes of the church states that there was a prophecy saying the church would lie in ruins two times, and this was because it was built on the Katarina mountain, where the victims of the Stockholm bloodbath had been burnt in 1520 (see p. 40). This supposedly caused the site to be eternally cursed.

# ERSTA COMMUNION WAFER BAKERY

*Where the body of Christ is baked*

*Erstagatan 1*
*Museum (free): Tuesday, Wednesday and Thursday, 11.30am–1.30pm*
*The bakery keeps normal office hours*

There are very few communion wafer bakeries in Sweden, but one of them is right in central Stockholm and has been running since 1909. The bakery is in the building immediately on your right as you

© Ersta Oblattageri

enter through the gate to the Ersta Deacon Society grounds, and you can get a good view of the baking process through the ground-level windows.

On the left-hand side stands a small museum (opened in 1983) commemorating the long history (170-plus years) of the Ersta deaconesses and nurses – with photographs, recreated historical hospital rooms and old uniforms on display.

Well into the 1980s, predominantly retired deaconesses worked at the bakery – pro bono. Today, most bakers are properly employed, but there are also volunteers (often elderly) with different backgrounds. It is the biggest producer of communion wafers in Sweden, churning out some four million wafers every year. All wafers are gluten-free and ecological, with the ingredients being potato starch, cornflour, rice flour and guar gum.

Making communion wafers in this manner has roots stretching to the ninth century. Back then, a wafer iron consisting of two rectangular pieces of metal were filled with enough dough for three to four wafers, and one of the plates had Christian symbols engraved that created a stamped pattern on the finished products. The wafers were baked over an open fire.

© Ersta Oblattageri

Ever since the start back in 1909, the Ersta bakery has however used electrical irons. The present ones can make 44 wafers at a time, but the pace of production looks relaxed rather than frantic.

## The bakery only sell their products to properly registered churches …

Most clients are Swedish congregations, but there are also foreign customers. Before you get any ideas about picking up a weird snack to amuse your friends with next time you have them over for tea, be advised that the bakery only sell their products to properly registered churches. Surplus money from sales goes to the charitable activities of the Ersta Deacon Society.

# TEATER DUR OCH MOLL

*Stockholm's smallest theatre*

*Fjällgatan 16–18*
*durochmoll.se*
*info@durochmoll.se*
*Metro: Slussen*

In a tiny cottage on Stigberget, a mountain on Södermalm, Teater dur och moll is Stockholm's smallest theatre.

Since opening in 1998 it has offered plays created especially to suit the premises, usually tales of women in historical times – for example dealing with the Swedish witchcraft trials in the 17th century. The actress Gen Hedberg runs most of the theatre's business, with help from a pool of professionals and enthusiasts. Especially impressive are the grotesque masks used.

There are only 20 seats, so watching a play here is a very intimate affair. No spectator will be more than 4 metres from the actors, meaning eye contact can be maintained in a unique way. Leaflets proudly proclaim it is 'the smallest theatre in the world!', which may or may not be true – but it is definitely the smallest of its kind in Stockholm, and probably also in Sweden.

The name of the street is Fjällgatan, with 'fjäll' indicating a type of great mountain – in reference to its high altitude (to find an actual fjäll, though, you have to go to the north of Sweden). Stigberget was once the gallow's hill, a grim place of execution. When the gallows were moved to Skanstull in the late 17th century, people started building houses here. No fancy houses, of course – as no one with money would want to live somewhere with a history like this – but wooden shacks. They were not long-lived, however, as the great fire of 1723 devoured them all, along with most other buildings in the parish.

After the fire, the present-day theatre was one of the first new buildings built on the ashes. A carpenter named Andersson bought the plot of land from a butcher and built himself a two-room cottage with a thatched roof facing the street. In the courtyard, he built a bakery. Andersson, his wife, three children and three maids all lived in the cottage itself. His wife ran a 'sylteri', a sort of unpretentious eatery serving cold cuts.

By 1756, the family had moved out, and the cottage toward the street became a rowdy tavern, Aline on the Mountain. For more than 50 years it remained a place of toasting, boasting and drunken feasting. Today, this is the building where the theatre is housed. It looks fairly similar to the way it did in 1805, when it was converted into a weight shop run by a man named Blåberg.

# CAPTAIN ROLLA MONUMENT

*The broken monument to a tragic aeronaut*

*Above Klevgränd*
*Metro: Slussen*

On the back of the popular entertainment establishment Mose-
backe is a peculiar monument to the daring aeronaut Captain
Rolla. You can only see it if you walk down the stairs on the back of
Mosebacke or if you approach from the street below.

Attached to the wall is a silhouette of an astonished audience, part
of the balloon, and the captain himself. The latter, however, has only
one of his legs remaining. The rest of the monument, by artist Rolf
Swedberg (1927–2008), has probably been broken by storm winds and
carried away – which is quite fitting.

Who was Captain Rolla (1870–1890), then? Born Victor Rolla in Vitebsk, Belarus, this young adventurer and acrobat trained under the aeronaut Charles Leroux in Tallin. Leroux drowned after a failed parachute jump. After being prohibited by local authorities in Helsinki to perform with balloon and parachute due to the risks, Rolla arrived in Stockholm in the spring of 1890. His act became an instant hit. In front of an audience at Mosebacke, he made three attempts to parachute from the balloon. The first, on 15 May, was a complete failure, with the balloon ending up in a shrubbery before he could jump. The second, on 18 May, saw him ascend to high altitude and climb down to detach the parachute – but he ended up tangled in its ropes, and it unfolded only shortly before he hit the water. The audience loved it.

During Captain Rolla's third ascent, on 29 May, he lost control of the balloon, and the wind carried him out to sea. Startled spectators saw him hovering as a small dot far away over the water for several hours before disappearing. The day after, his dead body was retrieved outside Ljusterö. The post-mortem revealed he froze to death before the balloon crashed into the water.

Mass media attention following the event was huge in Sweden and internationally. Some 50 or 60,000 people attended the funeral, making it one of the century's biggest, and popular songs praised the tragic figure of Captain Rolla. A wax cast was made of his face and used for a Rolla display, complete with balloon, at the Panoptikon wax museum in Stockholm (a local version of Madame Tussaud's in London). It remained in place until the museum closed in 1924, and the daring young aeronaut started to gradually fade from public consciousness.

On the 100th anniversary of his tragic death, the monument was installed at Mosebacke.

# THE BELLMAN HOUSE ⑨

*The home of a songwriter and his parodic Masonic order*

*Urvädersgränd 3*
*bellmanhuset.se*
*Guided tour the first Sunday of every month at 1pm*
*Metro: Slussen*

Owned by the quasi-Masonic order Par Bricole (see p. 87), the Bellman House offers an enthralling glimpse of 18th-century Stockholm and its teeming world of secret societies. It can be visited once a month (see opposite).

On the ground floor is the main lodge room of Par Bricole, with heavy doors decorated with metal grapes and leaves (symbolising the centrality of wine drinking in the order's activities).

Along the walls are the heraldic shields of the order's brothers, often with references to epicurean pleasures. A small door is decorated with a French horn, alluding to the importance of music. At the far end of the room is a painted backdrop featuring the Haga Park, while a table bears the all-seeing eye of God. Also on display on this floor are various staffs topped with carved bunches of grapes for ceremonial use, historical drinking horns and cups, and the lute of Bellman himself.

A celebrated poet and songwriter, Carl Michael Bellman (1740–1795) lived in the house during his peak productive years (1770–1774), when he wrote his most famous songs. The top floor features a reconstruction of Bellman's living quarters, and his death mask hanging next to a handsome green tiled stove.

Built by the farrier Adam Wollman in 1764, the premises are a well-preserved and piously renovated example of the period's architecture.

TEMPEL.                    19

*Han har nu tjent sin tid arbetat och fått lof.*

The eastern part of the plot of land was used as a herb garden, which remained until the early 20th century.

In 1938, Par Bricole bought the house and had it restored. It is shown to the public on the first Sunday of every month, with singers in period costume performing a potpourri of Bellman songs. The singers and guides are often quite eccentric Bellman fanatics, making this a very colourful and entertaining experience that cannot be recommended enough.

It is possible to book private showings of the house, at a cost of 2,000 SEK. You can also peek in through the windows whenever you like, and during late evenings you may catch a glimpse of inebriated Par Bricole brothers – wearing white tie outfits and order regalia – heading home from a lodge meeting.

## Par Bricole: A humorous order

Members usually interpret the name Par Bricole as meaning 'by chance'. The group started in 1779 as a circle of cheerful friends, including the famous Bellman. They met semi-regularly, more or less by chance, in various Stockholm taverns. Most were initiates of the Swedish Order of Freemasons.

One of them, Olof Kexél, started taking Par Bricole in a Masonic direction around 1780 by drawing up statutes, a degree system and initiation rituals – but all with a humorous twist, poking gentle fun at the period's Masonic trend and the many related secret groups springing up like mushrooms across the nation.

Bellman was instated as the official poet of the order, and several other illustrious poets also joined. Only men are allowed to become members and the order enjoys royal protection.

The emphasis has quite consistently been on bacchanalian shenanigans and long dinners with witty speeches and copious toasting (even if more mystically inclined ceremonial activities briefly almost gained the upper hand in the early 19th century). Presently, Par Bricole has lodges in Stockholm, Gothenburg, Vänersborg, Borås, Malmö, Jönköping, Sundsvall, and Örebro, with the Bellman House as the 'mother lodge'.

Among today's famous Par Bricole brothers is the culinary expert, cultural historian and general cult figure Edward Blom.

© Holger Ellgaard

# THE ALMGREN FACTORY

*An active textile factory in the middle of Stockholm*

*Repslagargatan 15A*
*kasiden.se*
*info@kasiden.se*
*Monday to Saturday noon–4pm*
*Entrance fee*
*Metro: Slussen*

**A** place of vibrant industrial history filled with fully functioning wooden machines, Almgren is surprisingly an active textile factory in the middle of Stockholm.

© Klas Nyberg

A couple of years ago, the last weaver retired – but the factory is now being used to apprentice three new weavers and, it is hoped, will be fully up and running again soon.

The house is intentionally narrow, being designed for daylight to flood in through the large windows on both sides in the era before electrical light.

Opened in 1833, the Almgren factory (K.A. Almgrens sidenväveri) predates the industrial revolution in Sweden, but existed right through the industrial era. Today, there is no real textile industry left in Sweden, as it has all long since moved to low-wage countries.

After getting tickets, begin your visit by heading up to the third floor, which houses an informative museum about the history of Almgrens. And what a long, illustrious history it is, with Almgrens, among many other things, probably being the oldest active officially appointed supplier to the royal court (since 1844). There is also an attention-grabbing display of fraternal sashes (from orders like The Swedish Order of Freemasons, Timmermansorden, and Par Bricole), all produced by Almgrens and having various mysterious metal insignia attached.

On the second floor, the weaving mill and its machines are close to how they looked more than 100 years ago, and most of the appliances still function. Many of them have pencil markings drawn by the women who once worked them. You can almost hear the thumping of the looms and the hushed voices of the weavers as you walk around. At Almgrens, the past remains very much alive.

---

Almgrens is the only active silk factory remaining in the Nordic countries.

---

## A trip to France to steal industrial secrets

The founder, K.A. Almgren, travelled to France in the 1820s to seek treatment for his tuberculosis, but his ulterior motive was to steal French industrial secrets. French silk factories were closed to foreigners to prevent this, but he learned the language so well that he managed to fool his way into one of the facilities employing the new, hyper-efficient jacquard loom. This machine used punch cards to lift the warp, drastically reducing the manual labour needed. The punch cards were the first step towards today's digital machines. Returning home, Almgren illegally smuggled dismantled jacquard mechanics with him and went into business in 1833.

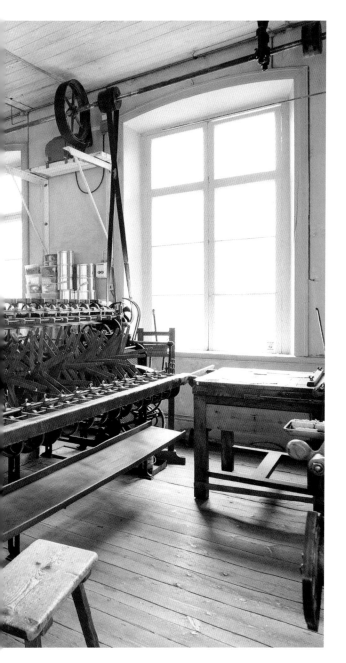

# MERMAID STATUES
# AT THE VAN DER NOOT PALACE

## *The bath of Melusine*

*Sankt Paulsgatan 21*
*Metro: Slussen or Mariatorget*

Above the door to the van der Noot Palace, two peculiar mermaid-like female figures can be seen. They are linked to an interesting story.

During the 19th century, when the palace stood temporarily empty and abandoned, strange rumours started circulating: It was said that it was forbidden to open a certain door in the palace. Behind it, a beautiful woman named Melusine took her bath every Saturday evening and was transformed into a frightening half-serpent creature. This story is based on an old French folk tale popularised in Sweden in the 18th and 19th centuries through cheap mass-market books.

It has been suggested these well-liked books, in combination with the striking mermaid doorway ornaments on the palace, gave rise to the rumours.

Designed by Mathias Spihler or Jean de la Vallé (or possibly both), the van der Noot Palace was built for the Dutchman Thomas van der Noot, who enjoyed a successful military career in Sweden during the country's so-called great power period.

As fate would have it, van der Noot fell during the battle of Stettin in 1677, only three years after the palace was finished. After his death, the Dutch delegation moved in and remained in the house for 100 years. They were followed by a church, a tobacco factory, a school, a gymnastic institute, and, finally, offices. At the start of the 20th century, there were plans to tear down the building. Luckily, it was bought in 1903 by Jean Jahnsson, a wealthy jeweller who restored it to its former glory. The pseudo-historical interior decoration dates from this time, and not from the time the house was built, as one might believe.

When it was later threatened by demolition, businessman Axel Wenner-Gren bought it and gave it to Sweden's *lottakårer* (an auxiliary defence organisation of the Swedish Home Guard, founded in 1924).

Today it is used as a conference centre and for parties. It is popular with university employees, and quite a few small academic conferences and thesis defence parties have been held there.

Around lunchtime it is possible to go in and have a look, as there is a lunch restaurant inside. Unfortunately, it is not open for lunch on Saturdays, so one would have to be a visitor to an event hosted there in order to go in and listen for the splashing of water when Melusine supposedly takes her Saturday bath and is transformed.

The palace is well worth a visit on a weekday anyway, and some of the other spaces may be open for viewing. The big library upstairs, with its green and gold panelling, is especially beautiful.

# JAS 39 GRIPEN CRASH MEMORIAL ⑫

*A memorial over a military embarrassment*

*Below the southern abutment of Västerbron at Långholmen*
*Metro: Hornstull*

One of the smallest memorials in Stockholm is a tiny metal sculpture of a paper plane crashing into the ground, below the southern abutment of Västerbron at Långholmen. It commemorates a

dramatic event on 8 August 1993, when the Swedish air force proudly wanted to show off their new multi-role combat aircraft (fighter, attack and reconnaissance), Gripen (The Gryphon).

To do so, they chose the Stockholm Water Festival, an annual street festival held between 1991 and 1999. However, the experienced test pilot, Lars Rådeström, lost control of the plane during a roll at low altitude due to problems with the computerised steering system and had to eject. The plane crashed near Västerbron, the bridge connecting Långholmen and Södermalm. Footage of the crash is dramatic, with a huge pillar of smoke rising from a grove of trees (there are several amateur films of the crash on YouTube). Amazingly, despite a crowd of thousands, only one person was injured – a woman hospitalised for three weeks with severe burns. With a minor change in course, things could have ended very badly indeed.

This was not the first crash for the heavily criticised Gripen project. In February 1989 a software malfunction (or pilot-induced oscillation, according to some) caused a plane (also piloted by Rådeström) to crash on a test field, a fiasco filmed by Swedish television. Of course, the second crash – right in the middle of the city! – resulted in a credibility crisis for the manufacturer and the army (in the long run, the damaged reputation of the JAS 39 Gripen was repaired, and later versions have been exported to several countries, and today it constitutes the backbone of the Swedish air force). After the crash, there were no more aerial displays at the Water Festival.

The choice of a paper plane, rather than the military plane involved, speaks to the pathetic dimension of what happened. Created by the sculptor Thomas Qvarsebo (who has made many pieces of public art throughout Stockholm and elsewhere) and erected in 1994, it was paid for by a hotel in Långholmen. There was a tree at the site that had been damaged by fire from the crash, but it was cut down in 2011.

© Tuomo Salonen / SIMFinnish Aviation Museum

# MINIATURE REPLICA OF MICKES SERIER, CD & VINYL

*An exact 1:12 scale replica of a shop*

*Långholmsgatan 20*
*Every day of the year, 11am–10pm*
*You can view the miniature through the window all day*
*Metro: Hornstull*

In the shop window of the legendary record and comic book shop Mickes Serier, there is a stunning little display likely unnoticed by most passers-by: An enthusiastic miniaturist has built an exact replica of the shop itself. Those who do notice are often so taken with it that they stick their heads in the door to ask who has built it, to which the owner can proudly respond that his sister made it for him.

Micke's sister, Ewa, crafted the piece as a gift for his 54th birthday on 17 November 2009. When Ewa and her partner arrived at the shop by car on the day in question, they took something big, cumbersome and covered in a blanket from the trunk – and Micke feared they had bought him an aquarium, which was the very last thing he wanted. He had no room and no time to take care of fish, as he was always in his shop working.

His distress was immediately transformed into speechless amazement when the cover was lifted, and his sister had made a replica of his shop!

It was exact down to the tiniest detail: cash register, shelves and tables filled with CDs and LPs, cardboard boxes and paper bags, functioning lamps. Made in a 1:12 scale, it took three years to create. Ewa began by taking photos of the shop in secret, with Micke's shop assistants being in on the plan. Though Ewa has no formal training in miniature-making, her work is masterly.

When Ewa asked on that November day where in his apartment Micke intended to put the model, he immediately decided it should instead be placed in the shop itself so that everyone could see it.

Open since 1996, the shop is renowned for its generous opening hours (until at least 10pm every day, often including even Christmas Eve) and the banter of the bohemian shopkeeper – Micke himself. Well-stocked with expensive vinyl rarities and bargain records, as well as comics and DVDs, the shop is one of the city's best spots for fairly priced collectibles. But the unique thing is the miniature replica.

# REIMERSHOLME VODKA BENCHES

*Have a seat in remnants of the vodka war*

*By the shore of Reimersholme*
*Open at all times of day*
*Metro: Hornstull*

On Reimersholme there are benches integrated into big vodka barrels, and cognac caskets on plinths. These are the remains of the so-called brännvinskriget (vodka war), where the attacking 'general' was a certain Lars Olsson Smith (1836–1913). At that time, Reimersholme was his base of operations and the barrels and caskets have been preserved to commemorate this.

Born to poor parents in southern Sweden, then adopted by a consul named Smith, Lars Olsson Smith went to school for only two years before starting various small businesses as a 10-year-old. In his young adulthood he built a fortune selling vodka. At a time when pretty much every male in Sweden was an alcoholic by today's standard (downing around 2 litres of vodka weekly!), booze was extremely lucrative.

Smith built a factory on Reimersholme to make high-quality vodka superior to that produced by the municipality monopoly. The name of his brand was Absolut Rent Brännvin, the precursor of today's Absolut Vodka. The monopoly only encompassed the Stockholm municipality, and Smith offered free boat rides to his factory on Reimersholme (at that time, not part of Stockholm) to circumvent it. Through price-dumping and aggressive marketing, he won the consumers over. Thus ended the first vodka war, and Smith became known as The Vodka King (Brännvinskungen).

However, the municipal monopoly later made new attempts to block Smith's business, leading the latter to publish a big ad in all the national newspapers bearing the heading 'Declaration of War'. Smith had established another factory, on Fjäderholmarna. Again, he offered free boat rides, with three ships going back and forth several times an hour.

Smith was a ruthless and shrewd businessman who became an active politician in the Swedish parliament, worked for social reforms and workers' rights, created cheap eateries for proletarians and learned seven languages in order to expand his business internationally. Among his most successful ventures was the export of vodka to Spain and Portugal. After many ups and downs, he died destitute in 1913.

## The Vodka King's occultist daughters

Both of Smith's daughters would go on to become high-profile occultists. His eldest daughter, Mary, became a princess through marriage with the Turkish diplomat Prince Jean Karadja Pasha, then turned to spiritualism after his death. She published many influential books on the topic. His youngest daughter, Lucie, married the nobleman Axel Lagerbielke, and edited occult journal *Framtidens folk* (*The People of the Future*).

# Kungsholmen – Normalm

| ① | LILLA HORNSBERG | 102 |
| ② | ARONSBERG JEWISH CEMETERY | 104 |
| ③ | INTERIOR OF ST GÖRANS GYMNASIUM | 106 |
| ④ | THE VESTIGES OF THE FORMER BIOGRAF DRAKEN CINEMA | 108 |
| ⑤ | SVEN HEDIN'S HOUSE | 110 |
| ⑥ | THE COLLECTIVE HOUSE | 114 |
| ⑦ | AIRSHAFTS OF THE KRONOBERG REMAND PRISON | 116 |
| ⑧ | COPPER FACES OF RÅDHUSET | 118 |
| ⑨ | PIPERSKA MUREN GARDEN | 122 |
| ⑩ | JUGENDSTIL DOORS OF GASVERKET | 124 |

⑪ MUSEUM OF PHARMACEUTICAL HISTORY 126

⑫ SKANDIA CINEMA 128

⑬ FENIXPALATSET 130

⑭ THE RELIEFS OF CENTRUMHUSET 132

⑮ UGGLAN PHARMACY 136

⑯ THE RELIEFS OF CENTRALPOSTHUSET 138

⑰ THE PHANTOM STATUE 140

⑱ THE SECRETS OF ADELSWÄRD HOUSE 142

⑲ KUNGSTRÄDGÅRDEN METRO STATION 144

⑳ RÖDA RUMMET AT BERNS 150

# LILLA HORNSBERG

*An 18th-century cottage, witness to a new-found respect for the past*

*Hornsbergs strand 22*
*Metro: Stadshagen*

By the Karlberg canal, the two picturesque 18th-century cottages preserved in an otherwise heavily modernised area offer fine examples of historical architecture.

The first of them, Lilla Hornsberg, was built in the 1760s and has sublime, irregular mouth-blown glass on the outer doors and robust iron hinges of a type common in the 18th century.

Looking in through one of the windows, you can see a blue and white tile stove from the same period. On the north side of the house is a blind window. The other windows retain the small size typical of the period, but were manufactured in the 1950s.

The building began its life as the guardhouse of Hornsberg Castle (the latter was torn down in 1890). It then became an inn called Fördärvet (The Corruption) in the mid-18th century. At the time it was close to a toll house. Peasants, having sold their goods at markets in the city, stopped there to spend their hard-earned cash on drink – to the chagrin of their wives waiting at home. You could drink on the premises

© Lilla Hornsberg

until the 1940s, when the severely dilapidated establishment was closed for sanitary reasons.

In the 1950s, the house was renovated and rented out as an office for literary societies. Much of the timber had to be replaced completely and, in an ambitious antiquarian effort, tiled stoves and doors from the collection of the Stockholm City Museum were installed.

When the society vacated the premises in 2011, the house stood empty for several years. Today, it is home to a Buddhist congregation offering courses in meditation and other activities. The landlord, Stadsholmen, owned by the city, had as a demand that the tenant should use the building for an activity with 'creativity as its point of departure' that is 'in line with the existent cultural historical and building antiquarian values' – for somewhat unclear reasons, they are apparently requirements fulfilled by Buddhism.

The renovation of Lilla Hornsberg marked a paradigm shift in the attitude toward historical buildings, and is thus also a monument over a new-found respect for the past in a period when knock-'em-down-and-replace was the usual practice.

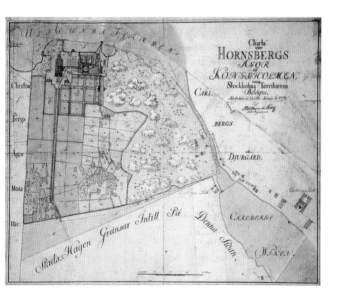

Next to the 1760s guardhouse is a slightly later building originally located in Södermalm but moved here in the 1950s (now a private residence).

# ARONSBERG JEWISH CEMETERY ②

*An atmospheric 18th-century cemetery in the middle of the city*

*Alströmergatan 47*
*Metro: Fridhemsplan*
*Not open. Excellent view of the gravestones from outside*

**A** few metres below today's street level, the old Jewish cemetery Aronsberg is an atmospheric 18th-century cemetery in the middle of

the city that encompasses 1,300 square metres. Although it is fenced in and not open to the public, you can get an excellent view of the gravestones from outside.

Its gravestones are beautiful patinated works of art. At the time it was instituted, the cemetery was located far from the hustle and bustle of the city, as Jewish custom dictates – a burial site should not be in proximity to dwelling places and is a holy place more sacred even than a synagogue. Today, however, it is surrounded by tenement buildings. A Jewish grave cannot be moved or reused, meaning the cemeteries fill up quite quickly (in a Christian cemetery, old graves no longer cared for by descendants are often moved and replaced with new ones).

The oldest grave in Aronsberg is from 1782 (one Beata Isaacson), and the newest from 1888. Over the years, 300 burials took place there, but not all have remaining markers. Many have withered away in the acidic Stockholm air and, sadly, some have also been vandalised by anti-Semites through the years – defaced with swastikas or even smashed to bits with sledgehammers.

Most of the gravestones are made from chalkstone or sandstone from Gotland, with a couple of exceptions in cast iron, and almost all carry inscriptions in Hebrew rather than the Latin alphabet. Dates are given in accordance with the Hebrew calendar, which draws on a Babylonian model.

Aronsberg's founder was Aaron Isaac (1730–1816), the first unbaptised Jew allowed to immigrate to Sweden. He was 43 years old and a married father of five at the time. He almost immediately set to work establishing a Jewish cemetery. He turned down an offer to use a plot of land in Klara cemetery, wanting to have a more secluded location. The site decided on was chosen both because it fulfilled this demand and because the ground was mostly postglacial clay – making it easy to dig graves.

## NEARBY
### Kronoberg Jewish burial site
A Jewish burial site almost as old is nearby Kronoberg. By 1787, the Jewish community in Sweden encompassed 150 individuals, and some of them felt that Aaron Isaac had become too authoritarian in his designated role as their representative. This group therefore created their own cemetery, also in Kungsholmen. Isaac was not impressed, contemptuously writing in his memoirs, "It is a small place beneath a mountain. When it rains, the filth from manure flows down onto the cemetery, and surely this construction has been more costly than mine." Eventually, both rival burial sites filled up, and the community acquired a much bigger plot of land in Norra begravningsplatsen (Solna).

# INTERIOR OF ST GÖRANS GYMNASIUM

## *A brutally brutalist 11-floor house*

*Sankt Göransgatan 95*
*The door to the main hall is locked, but there will usually be friendly students*
*coming and going who'll happily let you in to look around. A good view can*
*also be had through the window sections*
*Metro: Fridhemsplan*

I t has been called 'Stockholm's most beautiful building' by modernism enthusiasts. But a great many people cannot stand the huge, brutalist 1960s building that was formerly a school for 16–19-year-olds. Whatever your disposition, it will not leave a lukewarm impression. This is one of Stockholm's love-it-or-hate-it sights.

The architect Léonie Geisendorf (1914–2016) was inspired by her radical French colleague Le Corbusier, and St Görans Gymnasium is similar to his Unité d'Habitation – a type of building found in Berlin and several places in France. The idea was that many different functions would be collected in a single block, for example with jogging tracks on the roof. While this was not the case here, it borrowed heavily from the overall Unité d'Habitation style. At first, 1,000 girls studying housekeeping and sewing filled the premises, but 11 years later it became a broader practical education institution welcoming boys as well.

However, St Görans Gymnasium gradually deteriorated, with a lack of repairs and problems with ventilation causing it to be closed in 2008. The idea was to renovate it and reopen. But in the end, it turned out to no longer meet the demands put on a school. For a long period, the closed 11-floor building suffered repeated break-ins and vandalism, with only occasional official use as a location for films in need of a grimly brutalist setting.

Today, it has been turned into student housing and a day-care centre. Its architect, Léonie Geisendorf, 100 years old at the time, had many strong opinions regarding this process, remaining fiercely engaged in its fate pretty much all the way up to her death at 102.

The repetitive glass, black and concrete facade is not an uplifting sight to most eyes, but going in might (no promises!) change your mind. The main entrance hall looks more like a lavish, modernist theatre than an old school, with original 1960s lighting fittings, spiral staircases, geometrical, jagged greyscale stone floor intarsia – and lots of raw concrete. Another groovy detail is the wrought-iron railings with asymmetrical, musical note-like decorative patterns.

# THE VESTIGES OF THE FORMER BIOGRAF DRAKEN CINEMA

## *A dragon fountain and a neon sign*

*Fridhemsplan 27*
*The sign can be viewed at all times. The fountain can be viewed during the storage facility's opening hours: 6am–midnight*
*Metro: Fridhemsplan*

Atop Fridhemsplan number 27, the mighty green neon body of a dragon crouches in the darkness, claws clutching, yellow eyes staring, tongues of flame darting from its mouth. The beast used to guard a silver treasure – a silver screen in a cinema, to be precise. Now, however, it protects the rather more diverse contents of people's boxed-up personal goods in a storage facility. Even so, it still holds the old *Svensk Filmindustri* logotype in its claws and will remain in place due to its high value as a part of the city's cultural heritage.

An early example of a neon sign with simulated movement (the flames), it was drawn by the artist Rudolf Persson and constructed by neon master Ruben Morne. After sections of it gradually stopped functioning, the whole sign was renovated in 2012 (that is, replaced with a faithful replica).

In the former cinema foyer, a drinking fountain where water used to come streaming from the mouth of a bronze dragon into a shell, made by artist Gösta Fredberg, remains preserved. Anyone can go in for a look or to stroke its bronze scales. If you ask nicely, the friendly reception staff may even turn on the water. A true hidden gem.

Opened on 2 May 1938, Biograf Draken used to be a spectacular cinema palace with 1,125 seats. The screen curtain, designed by Isaac Grünewald, had dragon motifs in 135 colours. At the back of the main screening room was a telephone, which could be used to call a doctor from nearby St Göran's Hospital in case of medical emergencies. The name of this hospital ('St George's' in English), which opened in 1888, may be the reason for the name of the cinema – Saint George being a legendary dragon slayer.

In 1996, the cinema was closed – one of the last victims of the home video revolution. For a while it was used for Christian prayer meetings, which is somewhat ironic given that in the Bible the dragon is synonymous with Satan (as stated in Revelation 12:9), before finally ending up as a storage facility.

# SVEN HEDIN'S HOUSE

*An explorer's monument to himself*

*Norr Mälarstrand 66*
*The decorations are clearly visible through the entrance door*
*Metro: Rådhuset*

Among the forward-looking, modernity-embracing functionalist houses along the shoreline of Norr Mälarstrand, the building on number 66 sticks out like a sore conservative thumb. Designed in classicist style with heavy pillars flanking the front entrance, it was commissioned by explorer Sven Hedin (1865–1952), which is obvious when peeking in through the glass of the front door.

The stairway is filled with three-dimensional maps of Asia stretching along the right wall, and a relief of a Chinese temple along the left one. Above the temple, clouds depicted in Chinese style float against the background of the sky-blue wall. Further in, but also visible from outside, are painted decorative borders of camel riders, tents and guns.

All this refers to Hedin's achievements and adventures as an explorer, and the painted portions are probably based on his field drawings. Malicious comparisons have likened the overall aesthetic to that of a 1970s pizza parlour or a cheap Chinese restaurant.

Hedin lived here from 1935 until his death in 1952 in a triplex apartment on the top three floors, shared with his two unmarried sisters, who helped him with the daily chores.

A member of the Swedish Academy, Hedin was an international celebrity through his books about adventurous journeys through distant Central Asian lands – portraying himself as a sort of Indiana Jones. Knighted on 1 July 1902, he was the last Swede to receive this honour.

Some of his supposedly heroic deeds have later been questioned (for example, a rather pointless march through the desert that cost two lives), but most compromising was his close relationship to the Nazis.

During Hitler's youth, Sven Hedin was one of his favourite authors. The communist-hating Hedin would later give his full support to Nazi Germany, even delivering an enthusiastic speech at the opening of the 1936 Berlin Olympics. Hitler was very happy about having the backing of his hero and granted numerous private audiences to Hedin, who was a member of several Nazi organisations in Sweden and abroad (before and after World War II). Shortly after Hitler's suicide, he wrote an obituary praising his dear chum as one of the great men of world history. And, notoriously, he would attempt to raise toasts to Hitler during dinners even in 1949. Surprisingly, a crater on the moon was nonetheless named after Hedin as late as 1964.

# THE COLLECTIVE HOUSE

*A failed attempt at communal housing*

*John Ericssonsgatan 6*
*The building can be viewed from outside at all times. The food lift in Petite France can be seen during the bakery's opening hours: 7am–7pm, except Mondays (open until 6pm) and Saturday to Sunday (open until 5pm)*
*Metro: Fridhemsplan or Rådhuset*

Inside Stockholm's best French bakery, Petite France, food lifts can send food up to the apartments of the house. They are found next to the counter and adjacent to the kitchen. Why such a unique setup? The lifts are remnants of a radical example of Social Democrat utopian fantasy, the 1935 *Kollektivhuset* (The Collective House), where Petite France has been located since 2008.

The building has 57 functionalist apartments, all with angled little balconies with curved corners. The primary innovation was that trained in-house personnel, rather than the mothers themselves, would take care of (including at night, if need be) all children living there in ground-floor facilities, while a big central kitchen would rationalise cooking for the inhabitants and save space in the apartments. Meals were delivered via food lifts. Laundry could also be handled in a central launderette, and there were shafts on each floor where clothes could be sent down to it. A 21-person staff served the tenants, so they could be more efficient with their own work. Fittingly for something that was at heart a social experiment, in the 1950s the day care centre had a laboratory for child observation through a one-way mirror.

Plans for the building were drawn up by architect Sven Markelius in cooperation with Social Democrat Alva Myrdal (1902–1986). The latter's fight against nuclear arms earned her a shared Nobel Peace Prize in 1982, but she was also a eugenicist who in the famous book *Kris i befolkningsfrågan* (*Crisis in the Population Issue*, 1934), co-written with her husband Gunnar, argued for the economic rationality of a radical 'purging of highly unfit-for-life individuals' through a 'fairly merciless process of sterilisation', since 5 to 10 percent of the population could not 'make a contribution that morally justifies their lives'. Their cold and drastic suggestion was subsequently partially implemented by the government, which casts a sinister shadow over Myrdal's rationalistic concept for the building.

Many of the cultural radicals of the period moved in. According to a flippant contemporary remark, dropping a bomb on it would have eliminated a significant portion of the country's intellectual elite. Markelius himself lived in the building for a few years, but eventually relocated to a villa in posh Danderyd – the socialist utopia was apparently not a way of life appealing to its creators, and eventually the whole rationalistic-collectivist setup in the building was scrapped. But the food lifts remain.

# AIRSHAFTS OF THE KRONOBERG REMAND PRISON

## Science fiction-like brutalist design

*Bergsgatan 52*
*Metro: Rådhuset*

You will not be able to enter the remand prison in Kungsholmen without an invitation, or if you have done something wrong and are being taken there handcuffed. But you can enjoy the amazing, science fiction-like brutalist, oversized ventilation shafts outside it by Lars Englund.

Born in 1933, Englund was the subject of a major exhibition at the Museum of Modern Art in Stockholm in 2005 and has also exhibited to great acclaim in Venice, Paris, Warsaw, and New York. Most Swedes have carried around works by Englund in their wallets without being aware of it – as he designed the old Swedish 50 öre and 1 crown coins.

Englund's pioneering work in the 1960s employed industrial materials like plastic, rubber, and concrete when most of his Swedish peers were still stuck with more traditional choices. In an international context, this phase of his parallels the experiments of US minimalists around the same time, who used similar modern materials in nonfigurative works – though correspondences to baroque sculpture have also been pointed out.

The materials themselves have often shaped Englund's artistic style with, for example, swelling, distended rubber bodies. Responsible for over 40 pieces of public art, Englund's expressive yet restrained works are frequently unearthly in their cross-pollination of the organic and the geometrically abstract.

They also tend to add an intriguing, strange quality to buildings that might otherwise have been too muted, which is very much the case here. Unlike similar structures like Blåkulla in Solna and the Stockholm University campus in Frescati, the 1975 extension of the old Police House buildings has not attempted a mild blue colour to match the sky. Instead, the glass plating has different tones of brown and brownish pink – suitably stern for such a building, and in fact much more aesthetically consistent than lame attempts to take the edge off brutalism and make it pleasant (something of an oxymoron – it's not supposed to be cosy!).

The plating is held in place by small, discreet clips, and the colour shifts in interesting ways depending on the weather. The complex is given life and added interest by the air shafts, which you can walk up to and listen to the sound of the air flowing through them – something that in a sense makes this not just a visual and tactile sculpture, but also a sound sculpture.

# COPPER FACES OF RÅDHUSET

*Symbols of punishment?*

*Scheelegatan 7*
*Monday to Friday 8am–4pm*
*Metro: Rådhuset*

Rådhuset, the Stockholm Court House, is a place Stockholmers will typically only visit if they are involved in a trial, or if they are getting married in a civil ceremony. This means most of them have never set foot there. However, the building is an intriguing place, filled with quirky little secrets.

Taking five years to build, and finished in 1915, Rådhuset is one of the high points of Swedish national romantic architecture, with many references to the buildings of the Wasa Age (1523–1654).

On the north side, toward Kungsholmsgatan, is a mysterious sealed entrance with a lantern next to it. It used to lead to the chamber of 'Sterbhusnotarien', the person who handled questions concerning the estates of the deceased, a now defunct type of official. The text on the stone by the door is erased, and it is not known what it once said.

In the stones fitted around the main entrance, look for the seven deadly sins depicted in expressive granite miniature figures by Gustaf Sandberg (1876–1958).

But even more captivating are the faces on show when the outer portal is closed: four copper faces with the appearance of iron masks full

© Holger Ellgaard

of studs, like the top of an iron maiden or the battle mask of a medieval warrior, sculpted by Gustaf and his brother, Aron Sandberg. Exactly what the symbolism is remains unclear, though it might, like many of the other decorations, refer to some type of punishment (the iron maiden, or the myth of a prisoner with an iron mask spread by Voltaire).

In the entrance hall are the impressive 'Valans pelare' (The Pillar of the Seeress), a massive column carved from red Vätö granite and weighing 27 tonnes. It portrays the ancient Norse gods holding 'ting' (that is, a gathering where the governing body resolves disputes and passes laws) under the world tree Yggdrasil.

A sterner symbol of justice is the statue 'Kopparmatte' (Copper Matthew) on the second floor, a copy of a 17th-century original depicting a bearded man wielding a whip – reminding criminals they will get what is coming to them.

> It is also possible to attend the daily open court proceedings. An underground walkway connects with the Stockholm Police House, so criminals can be moved securely.

© Holger Ellgaard

Inside the main entrance is a spectacular, medieval-style frosted-glass and wrought-iron lamp, which is a three-dimensional version of the castle found in Stockholm's medieval city weapon. The same castle is carved from stone on the portal toward Scheelegatan.

© Frankie Fouganthin

# PIPERSKA MUREN GARDEN

*The baroque garden of a secretive lodge*

*Scheelegatan 14*
*Monday to Friday 8am–5pm*
*Metro: Rådhuset*

The attractive yet austere, strictly geometrical baroque garden in front of the Piperska Muren building is filled with statues, some of which have nautical motifs. These are probably linked to the symbolism of the mysterious Coldinu Order, whose mother lodge is located in the house. Several other secretive orders also hold their lodge meetings there.

At the same time, the premises are used as a conference centre and for private parties – meaning you can access it quite easily by simply asking to look around with the purpose of renting a room for an event (or just asking nicely in a more honest fashion). There is, however, nothing very esoteric about the rooms.

Originally built as a summer residence for count Carl Piper at the end of the 17th century, it was bought in 1765 by the Amaranter Order, who sold it on to the Coldinu Order in 1807.

© Frankie Fouganthin

## What is the Coldinu Order?

Supposedly, the saga of the very mysterious Coldinu Order stretches back to a medieval order of seafarers around the Mediterranean Sea and is linked to, as an internal publication from 1919 puts it, 'one of the biggest events in World history', giving no information about what this event is. Brought to Sweden in 1757 by Swedish navy captain Carl Biörnberg, today it remains active only in Sweden and Finland, but the Swedish division also briefly operated a branch in the Swedish Caribbean colony St Barthélemy (under Swedish rule 1784–1878). A large portion of the Coldinu Order's brothers have come from high nobility, often with close ties to the Royal Court. This is still the case: its present Grand Master belongs to one of the oldest noble families in the country. A famous non-noble member was the composer Hugo Alfvén (1872–1960), who produced a choir piece for the order in 1955. It is notable that the Swedish founder, Captain Biörnberg, also had a strong interest in music and was a member of the Royal Swedish Academy of Music. The order has installed enigmatic crosses mounted on poles along Swedish coast lines, the significance of which is a secret to outsiders.

## Other orders at Piperska Muren

Other orders also hold their lodge meetings at Piperska Muren. Among them is the Svea Order – a patriotic, Christian initiatory society with 10 degrees that also has a section open to women. Its initiations are intended to bestow knowledge about the culture of ancient Sweden, with names like the 'Freya Degree' (third degree initiation for women).

# JUGENDSTIL DOORS OF GASVERKET

## Tolkienesque turn-of-the-century copper doors

*Torsgatan 22–28*
*The interior is closed to the public, but one of the most interesting rooms can be seen through a window*
*Metro: T-Centralen or St Eriksplan*

On a stretch of street between T-Centralen and St Eriksplan that fairly few pedestrians walk, an architectural masterpiece stands half forgotten.

Built between 1904 and 1906, it originally housed the Stockholm gasworks and water company. Most impressive are the massive double copper doors on Torsgatan 22, with Jugendstil/art nouveau torches in relief, looking like the gates to a Tolkienesque elven or dwarven kingdom.

Sadly, they will remain locked no matter how many times you say the magic word 'Mellon' (the password to the gates of Moria in *Lord of the Rings*). Above the door, the patron saint of Stockholm, St Erik, looks down on passers-by like a melancholy elf king framed by oak leaves and acorns. The doors are a very tactile experience if you run your hands over the beautifully cast decorations. The burning torch motif recurs on the copper roof above.

Initially, the building also contained apartments, but these were turned into offices in the 1970s. It was designed by the super-productive architect Ferdinand Boberg (1860–1946), who had at that point in his career gained the exclusive right to do all 'technical buildings' for the city. In the same year, 1906, Boberg created similarly-inspired decorations for the Brunkeberg power station (today moved to Tulegatan 13), where a sort of goddess of electricity with a halo of lightbulbs and cables adorns the portal.

Internally, the building has undergone extensive renovations by the property company Castellum that owns it today. Most of it has been quite ruthlessly modernised into anonymous office spaces, with few original details preserved, aside from in the spaces where cultural heritage law has demanded otherwise. The latter include the office of the head engineer (where a heist scene in the legendary Swedish crime comedy *Jönssonligan* was shot in 1981, serving as the office of the nefarious millionaire Wall-Enberg) and the boardroom, neither of which are open to the public.

You can get a good look at the former gas token hall, where Stockholmers used to buy the tokens for their gas meters, through the ground-floor windows to the right of the copper doors. It has artfully decorated wooden panelling and a stucco ceiling.

# MUSEUM OF PHARMACEUTICAL HISTORY

*Bizarre medicines and a baking table for opium*

*Wallingatan 26A*
*To book, call 08-723 50 00 or send an e-mail: historiker@apotekarsocieteten.se*
*Open by appointment only*
*A group of up to 15 people may visit the museum together with a pharmacist guide for a fee*
*Metro: Odenplan*

© Apotekar Societeten

Things like special cigarettes for asthmatics and radioactive water for treatment of afflictions make you happy you live in the present time, not 100 years ago. Such bizarre medicines, and many other fascinating items, can be found at the Museum of Pharmaceutical History, one of the more obscure and amusing museums in Stockholm, located in a small, old building.

Its 350 square metres are filled with imaginative pharmacy signs, parts of the interiors of historical pharmacies, jars and tools – scales, mortars and pestles, pipettes, test tubes, and so on – from the 18th century to the present time.

Some items on display are quite gruesome, such as the special box to keep leeches in, with damp gauze and air holes to keep the little bloodsuckers alive. This was not just to preserve them on their way to be applied to a patient, but for them to be reused on other patients, which may not seem very hygienic.

On display is also a special baking table for opium. The black opium dough was put under a rolling pin and turned into small cakes stamped with the word 'OPIUM'. Just for the record, you can no longer buy these black cakes in Stockholm's pharmacies.

Early examples of pharmacy from the 16th and 17th century show how it was believed that all plants and trees, being created by God, had medicinal properties.

For example, Swedish pharmacists at that time suggested that since the scales of pine tree cones resembled teeth, they could cure toothache, whereas kidney beans, of course, were effective against maladies affecting the kidneys. Those with blue eyes were to use the blue cornflower for eye water, and so on.

© Apotekar Societeten

# SKANDIA CINEMA

*Spectacularly decorated opulent 1920s cinema*

Drottninggatan 82
*If the cinema is open, you can usually have a look*
*Metro: Hötorget*

U sed mostly for special events in recent decades, and thus less known to younger people, the 1920s cinema Skandia offers one of Stockholm's most beguiling period interiors.

The screening room has an arched dark blue ceiling intended to look like a night sky. Originally, it had white glass globes hanging from it to emulate planets. Graeco–Roman and Christian mythology is represented in the decorations, as are the mythological figures of contemporary Hollywood – in the shape of stars like Harold Lloyd, Charlie Chaplin and Mary Pickford.

On the right and left sides of the stage, respectively, are gilded wooden statues of Adam and Eve. Adam's torso has a mark from a notice attached to it with adhesive tape when a Pentecostal church rented the premises for some years in the 1980s. One might wonder what the Pentecostals thought of the railing on the stairs, decorated with unholy-looking brass serpent heads.

As it was built in the 1920s, Skandia originally screened silent films, which meant it had a Wurlitzer theatre organ. Aside from music, it could produce sound effects in accordance with what was occurring in the films. It was played by an organist in a white dinner jacket, and a mechanism could raise him slowly through the floor. The old organ space remains, but the instrument is in the former R1 reactor (see p. 292).

The house itself was built in 1854 and, to find room for a cinema, the backyard had to be co-opted for the salon. Initially handled by architect Ragnar Hjorth, the project was handed over to his up-and-coming colleague Gunnar Asplund (with help from Uno Åhrén and Kjell Westin), who created this masterpiece between 1922 and 1923. At the time he was also working on his most famous creation, the Stockholm Public Library, that would make him an international star.

Asplund was well connected in the art world, and brought in many of his artist friends to help decorate Skandia. Among them were future stars like Leander Engström (who did the ceiling paintings in the stairs), Stig Blomberg (reliefs in the vestibule) and Einar Forseth (friezes, putti). Prominent critics of the period hailed the result a masterpiece.

In its opening year, Skandia had room for 852 patrons, but today only for 532, as the space between the rows has been increased (from 7 decimetres to as much as 11 in some rows) for better comfort. It was recently bought by the Stockholm Film Festival.

# FENIXPALATSET

*A former 'palace of sin' turned church*

*Adolf Fredriks kyrkogata 60*
*The building can be visited on Sundays around lunchtime*
*Metro: Hötorget*

Fenixpalatset (The Phoenix Palace) is an apt name, as the building has 'died' and been resurrected many times and is now a church. It retains many interesting details from its raucous glory days, such as carved phoenixes that remain in several places as a reminder of the past in what was once a site of debauchery and prostitution.

The house was built in 1912, with the initial concept being a sports palace featuring roller skating, bowling and billiards. However, it soon became more of an entertainment stage focusing on concerts with jazz greats like Duke Ellington and Coleman Hawkins. All was not jazz, though: between 1912 and 1940, the premises hosted everything from dancing to beauty contests and women's suffrage meetings. Throughout the building there were several smaller establishments, such as an oyster bar and a specialised beer bar.

After some economic slumps, the venue's name was changed to Kaos (Chaos) in 1930, and it once more drew huge audiences. Up to 1,000 guests could be squeezed in, and among them were women selling their bodies – earning Fenixpalatset a reputation as a 'Palace of Sin'. The outbreak of World War II brought the partying to an instant halt. The French fine dining restaurant could no longer procure the necessary exclusive ingredients, artists could not travel freely, half of the staff were called up for army service, and the whole economy took a dive.

In 1940, a Pentecostal church bought the building, and converted the main hall into a place of worship. The congregation only had 200 members, so there was plenty of space for them in the 5,000-square-metre building. Luckily, there is no theological reason in Pentecostalism for any particular decorations, as a church is only considered a shell to contain the faithful celebrating God's omnipresence. Thus, the Pentecostals left pretty much all decorative details as they were.

On Sundays, you can visit the church service in the three-storey main hall, with its beautiful, gilded balconies and light flowing in through the domed glass ceiling. There are several smaller rooms that can be rented for conferences and events, for example the Turkish Salon (which isn't all that Turkish in style but features a wall painting probably intended to depict a landscape in Turkey), once used as a smoking room.

# THE RELIEFS OF CENTRUMHUSET  ⑭

*Humorous reliefs about life in early 20th-century Stockholm*

*Kungsgatan 32–38*
*The decorations and stairs can be viewed all day*
*Metro: Hötorget*

I n spite of being on one of the busiest intersections of Stockholm, Centrumhuset has subtle, amusing decorations most people never notice. Along the building, many small burnt clay relief plaques depict life in Stockholm. They were sculpted by the brothers Aron (1873–1959) and Gustaf Sandberg (1876–1958), who shared a studio on Humlegårdsgatan 8 for 50 years. Aron was also well known as a furniture designer and interior decorator.

The many reliefs, near-hidden by blending into the building so well, tell little stories about life in early 20th-century Stockholm: a young girl quenching her thirst at a drinking fountain (some of these fountains remain in place, but few are still functioning); a mother holding an umbrella over her babycart; a man kissing a woman on the neck from behind (or is it Dracula biting one of his victims in the throat?); a grim, witch-like figure raising her hand, with the caption 'Portvakt' (gatekeeper) – a function common in Stockholm apartment buildings back in the day, and in fact in existence well into the 1990s in some houses; a newspaper boy peddling his wares; a bricklayer carrying his materials; a cyclist in a striped outfit; a chimney sweep standing on a roof; a construction worker drilling in the ground; a balloon seller; a small child reaching for an ornate door handle; a mother shielding her infant from a goblin, or possibly a dog; a saluting cub scout; a sabre-armed traffic police officer directing cars and pedestrians. Plus many more.

The building itself, built between 1929 and 1931 and designed by Cyrillus Johansson (1884–1959), is also interesting, with its characteristic concave corner. Stylistically, it marks the transition from 1920s neoclassicism to functionalism, with a touch of German brick-expressionist style. Created as a space for shops and offices, it was the workplace of some 3,000 individuals when it opened in 1931 and used as much electricity as the entire town of Alingsås.

# NEARBY
## *The stairs of Centrumhuset*

A fascinating feature is the granite stairs (probably also a Johansson design) on the right side of the building's exterior, leading up to Malmskillnadsgatan, constructed as an optical illusion to make them appear longer than they are. At the foot, the stairs are 3 metres wide, narrowing to 2 metres at the top.

# UGGLAN PHARMACY

*Sweden's oldest pharmacy*

*Drottninggatan 59*
*Monday to Friday 10am–7pm, Saturday to Sunday 11am–5pm*
*Metro: Hötorget*

The Ugglan (Owl) Pharmacy is sometimes called the oldest pharmacy in Sweden, in the sense that it has been in the same premises since it opened in 1798 (there are others that started out considerably earlier but have moved to different locations). It is also gloriously well-preserved.

When first opening at Hötorget 1 in 1761, it was known as The Armoured Owl. This name was shortened to just The Owl. In 1798 it moved to its present premises on Drottninggatan. Pharmacies had animal names because animals were connected to different positive traits in medieval symbolism and because animal parts were a prominent part of older medicines.

A beautiful vertical neon sign spells out APOTEK. You enter through a narrow doorway flanked by tall cast iron columns, with a gilded owl clasping a snake in its claws above it (probably a symbol of medical learning defeating the snake of illness). The serpent may also be a reference to Asklepios, the Greek god of healing, whose attribute is a serpent-entwined rod (and in whose temples sacred serpents were kept). There are also several owls inside, for example an impressive specimen carved in wood spreading its wings above a mirror.

Modified and renovated several times through the years, the latest major makeover was in 1993. It retains the look it had in the 1890s, when most of the shelves, counters, and the ceiling paintings were created. The woodwork is primarily mahogany, a rainforest tree now deemed environmentally unsound to harvest – meaning new additions and replacements have been made of the similar-looking khaya wood from West Africa.

Other highlights include the chequered black and white floor and the beautifully painted ceiling with flower and medicinal herb motifs. The counters have marble tops, and there are old scales and brown glass bottles.

## A haunting ghost?

On 30 November 1868, a statue of King Charles XII was inaugurated in nearby Kungsträdgården. The well-known author August Blanche was supposed to give a speech, but felt poorly on his way to the event, and sought help in the pharmacy – where he died of a heart attack. This has naturally led to stories of Blanche's ghost haunting the house.

The carved wooden owl (wearing a breastplate) originally used as a sign is today part of the Nordiska Museet collection.

# THE RELIEFS
# OF CENTRALPOSTHUSET

*The Castle of Letters*

*Vasagatan 28–34*
*The lobby can be visited during normal office hours, and the exterior at any
time of day*
*Metro: T-Centralen*

Filled with playful and neglected details alluding to postal matters, the former main branch of the Swedish Postal Service (Postverket, in existence 1636–1994, but now replaced by the much detested Danish-Swedish corporation PostNord) ceased being a post office in the mid-1990s.

This resulted in this wonderful building largely fading from public consciousness in spite of its central location.

Built between 1899 and 1903, it was designed by Ferdinand Boberg (1860–1946), after a competition where five architects anonymously submitted proposals. Boberg was inspired by Vadstena castle, a medieval fortress in the south of Sweden. Boberg also designed furniture and glassware in a Jugendstil/art nouveau idiom, and this style is reflected in the fantastic decorations carved in the pinkish-red sandstone running along the building's exterior.

It features messenger pigeons, depicted in a mildly delirious turn-of-the-century style, flying over well-known Swedish landmarks, and is something you can spend quite a while studying in detail and marvelling at.

The building, encompassing some 30,000 square metres of office space, was featured on Swedish stamps issued in 1903 and 1974. Between 1930 and 1938, a functionalist extension was added, designed by Erik Lallerstedt. It is connected to the older building with two bridge-like structures across Klara norra kyrkogata, decorated with a strict grid pattern underneath.

In 2004, the National Property Board (Statens Fastighetsverk) bought the building, and various government ministries moved in. It is also an evacuation resource for the government in case of emergency, and thus a classified protected object (Skyddsobjekt).

The former counter for buying stamps is today the reception desk of the office hotel renting most of the building, while the rest of the im-

pressive main hall – with its soaring ceiling and colonnades decorated with the coats of arms of the Swedish regions – serves as a vast flexidesk office landscape. The many glimmering computer screens and busy atmosphere can be seen as a depressing testament to the privatisation of Swedish public services and public buildings, or as an example of the strong Swedish entrepreneurial spirit, depending on your disposition.

# THE PHANTOM STATUE

*Sweden's favourite obscure American comic book hero*

*Järnvägsparken*
*Metro: T-Centralen*

In a seldom-visited, tiny park squeezed between the Central Station and a motorway stands a 7-metre-tall statue paying tribute to a comic book hero recognisable to most older Swedes – but not to most foreign visitors or younger locals.

The hero in question is The Phantom, created by Lee Falk (more famous, probably, for his other comic character, Mandrake the Magician) in 1936.

The Phantom is based in the jungle of a fictional African country and has cultivated a legend about being immortal. Only his confidantes in a tribe of pygmies know the costume has in fact been handed from father to son for 22 generations. When he visits a city, he uses his family name (Mr Walker, which also becomes an allusion to his supposed immortality – 'The Ghost Who Walks') and wears a hat and an overcoat. Falk's hero preceded better-known competitors like Superman (1938) and Batman (1939) and was the first to wear the mask with no visible pupils that later became a superhero staple.

Erected in 2014, the statue of The Phantom in his city outfit was made by the artist Jan Håfström (born in 1937, and a four-time representative of Sweden at the Venice biennale). The Phantom has featured prominently in his pop art for a long time, but this is his first three-dimensional version. Håfström has described the running figure as also being symbolic of how his own father rushed by, and a parallel can be drawn to the hurried people passing though the Central Station.

The sculpture consists of two painted, joined-together aluminium silhouettes (weighing almost 2,000 kilos). Depending on the angle you view it from, it will look like Mr Walker is either running or falling. Characteristic of the simplified style of classic Phantom artist Wilson McCoy (1902–1961), the check pattern on the figure's overcoat is completely vertical/horizontal no matter how the garment moves.

The Phantom was never very popular in the US, but became a big hit in Sweden. Since the 1960s, Swedes have written and illustrated a sizeable portion of the comics. In the 1980s, a blue Phantom soda and Phantom candy were popular. There was even milk featuring The Phantom on the cartons (he is teetotal and prefers milk when visiting bars), and for over 20 years there existed a Phantom theme park in Eskilstuna. The comic is still around, but nowadays with a more modest edition.

# THE SECRETS
# OF ADELSWÄRD HOUSE

*A crest and a former baronial crown*

*Drottninggatan 2*
*Private, can only be viewed from the outside*
*Metro: Gamla stan or T-Centralen*

This grand 1890 house was built for the baron and industrialist Theodor Adelswärd (1860–1929). Though the family has not owned it for a long time, their crest is still prominently displayed on the facade, and the baronial crown is on the door handles.

Initially intended to be reminiscent of a Venetian palace, a change of course took place during the planning process for the house and it ended up as an eclectic interpretation of Swedish baroque architecture.

Theodor Adelswärd did not use Adelswärd House for very long. From 1907 to 2019 it contained, in succession, the Danish embassy, a bank office and the headquarters of a venture capitalist company. In 2019, it was bought by the Swedish State for 550 million Swedish crowns (a record price per square metre for an office building in Stockholm). In spite of these many different owners, the house is still known as Adelswärd House.

An interesting part of the family's history is the scandal of the so-called "black masses" (see opposite).

© 199jpcma

## The black masses of Baron Jacques

The Adelswärd family name was tainted by an unsavoury "occult" scandal 13 years after the house was finished. Theodor Adelswärd's brother, Adolf, was Sweden's military attaché in Paris, and there he spent much time with his young French relative Baron Jacques d'Adelsward-Fersen (1880–1923, note the Frenchified spelling of the family name). In 1902, Jacques also visited Sweden. He was an extravagant dandy, who wrote morbid, decadent poetry – but this did not prepare his Swedish relatives for what was to come. In the summer of 1903, Theodor received word from Adolf that Jacques had done something horrible. He wrote of "the awful scandal in which local newspapers now revel, and in which our name is dragged in the dirt thanks to Jacques who has brought shame and dishonour upon it". The infamous *affaire d'Adelsward* revolved around what the press called "black masses" – supposedly Satanist ritualistic homosexual orgies in Jacques' flat, involving underage boys. In fact, it appears that what took place was some sort of *tableaux vivants*, with a love/death theme (involving roses and a skull). Contemporary experts in the occult were sceptical of the claims regarding "Satanism", but the press stuck with them as they made for good copy. Swedish newspapers also reported, gleefully, on the "Satanist scandal" caused by an Adelswärd, much to the noble family's chagrin. After a dramatic trial, Jacques eventually ended up in exile on Capri, where he would take his own life in 1923 – according to some sources by taking an overdose of cocaine dissolved in a glass of champagne.

# KUNGSTRÄDGÅRDEN METRO STATION

*A delirious postmodern dream with a unique eco system*

O nly those who live along the blue metro line tend to get off at this station, as it is so close to the more convenient main hub T-Centralen (where all lines intersect). But this final stop is an amazing art installation, and home to peculiar flora and fauna, which is well worth anyone's time.

You can easily spend an hour at the station, looking for tiny spiders, peculiar moss and fungi, strange stalactites, bizarre sculptures, and just generally soaking up the otherworldly, surreal atmosphere.

It is best experienced late on a weekday night, when there are few passengers.

Between 1643 and 1825, the lavish palace Makalös (Incomparable) stood above the present station. It burnt down in November 1825. Tribute was paid to this by incorporating casts of many of the decorations from the palace in the metro station when it opened in 1977, meaning that you can marvel at the grotesque casts of decorative faces (mascarons) along the platform walls.

The station revels in postmodern bricolage style. In a fanciful portrayal of an archaeological dig site, you walk above a deep trench filled with antique columns and building fragments provided by the Stockholm City Museum, as well as a fountain, sprawling ivy and two massive gas lights (taken from the old gas works on Torsgatan) now lit up with blue neon lights. On each side of the trench stands a statue, representing architecture and painting, respectively.

The Italian bricklayers supposedly miscalculated the planned pattern on the floor, but the artist Ulrik Samuelson (born 1935) solved this by

© Arild Vågen

adding a barrel of oil spilling out over the platform – possibly a reference to the Soviet oil tanker Tsesis that leaked 1,000 cubic metres into the ocean outside Stockholm in 1977.

More certain is that the nuclear symbols painted on the ceiling allude to the 1986 Chernobyl incident, when the winds carried dangerous radioactive particles to Sweden.

A sculpture that looks like a petrified tree trunk, meanwhile, serves as a reminder of the so-called 'Battle of the Elms' in 1971, when angry Stockholmers clashed with police over plans to cut down thirteen 100-year-old elm trees to build the station (the elms were preserved).

Three guardian statues – including the god of war – installed in different locations throughout the station are reproductions of the 17th-century originals on the roof of the House of Nobility, now banished below ground.

> At 29.3 metres below ground, Kungsträdgården metro station is the deepest in Stockholm, and the only one to have completely untreated mountain as its walls.

© Arild Vågen

## An exceptional eco system

Kungsträdgården metro station has a unique eco system. Firstly, this is the only place in Northern Europe where the 2-mm spider *Lessertia dentichelis* can be found (possibly having hitched a ride with foreign machines used to build it). It was discovered by chance in 1980, when a spider specialist got off a train here. Usually found in caves, mines, and catacombs in more southern countries, it enjoys the raw granite and trickling water of the metro station. Secondly, in 2012, scientists found thriving *tuffkuddmossa* (*Eucladium verticillatum*), an obscure type of moss which has not been seen in Stockholm since the 1930s. Thirdly, a previously unknown fungus with a unique DNA structure was found growing on the walls in 2016.

A final mystery is the stalactites that have appeared in the tunnels, something that would normally require chalkstone or marble walls (not granite, like here). Scientists have no explanation for this at present.

# RÖDA RUMMET AT BERNS

*Neo-Gothic bohemian haunt*

*Näckströmsgatan 8*
*If you ask nicely at the front desk, you can usually go up and look at the Red Room (unless an event is taking place there), and you can rent it for dinners or events*
*Metro: T-Centralen*

O ne of Sweden's most famous novels, *Röda Rummet* (*The Red Room*, 1879) by August Strindberg (1849–1912), was named after a chambre separée popular with the fledgling bohemians of the period. Amazingly, the room is still preserved, as is much of the rest of the building, and the Strindberg family association (släktförening) often hold gatherings there on the author's birthday, 22 January.

Its interior bears testament to the 19th-century infatuation with medieval Gothic architecture, being all pointed little arches and stained glass. The room is not big, being only 40 square metres, with capacity for 20 seated guests. For events, it is often combined with the adjacent mirror hall (Spegelsalen), which can take another 70 or so people.

© Niklas Nyman

Strindberg's novel was based on actual events and people, and the Röda Rummet really was where the author, a very angry young man indeed, discussed art theory and radical politics with his peers. According to the novel, it served as a bachelor club for all of Stockholm, where one went to drink, smoke, and, above all, engage in heated debates. Given today's prices there, it might seem surprising that penniless freethinkers could afford to get drunk on the premises. Both similar and dissimilar crowds have come and gone there over the more than 140 years that have passed, and there was a 1980s revival of its bohemian reputation but today it has more of a leaning towards corporate patrons.

The Red Room is located in Berns, and was opened in 1863 by the entrepreneur Robert Berns in an effort to challenge the established entertainment institutions. Berns competed by providing knife throwers, theatre plays with monkeys as actors, Chinese fire-eaters, the weight-lifter Strong Arvid, the Arabian aerial acrobats Beni-Zug-Zug, and Sweden's first cancan performances. In the 1890s, jugglers, magicians, and escape artists drew crowds to Berns. Later, Sweden's first Chinese restaurant, Berns Asiatiska, opened there. Over the years, Bern's shifted owners many times, and its fortunes varied wildly, with the venue often teetering on, or falling into, bankruptcy.

The Red Room remains a somewhat hidden, exclusive part of today's Berns (which encompasses restaurants, nightclubs and a hotel) – a singular gem for those with an interest in cultural and literary history.

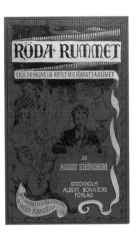

© Unknown source, Public domain, via Wikimedia Commons

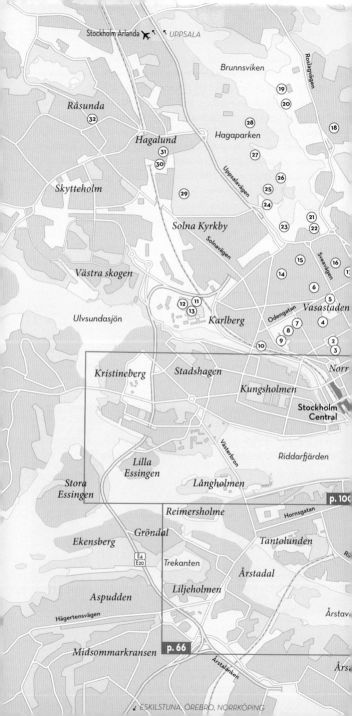

# North-West

1. INSCRIPTION IN THE BRUNKEBERGSTUNNELN     154
2. SWEDENBORG CHURCH     156
3. LODGE OF THE KNIGHTS TEMPLAR     160
4. THE GHOST CASTLE'S COLLECTION     162
5. THE STORYTELLING ROOM     170
6. ANTHROPOSOPHICAL LIBRARY     172
7. THE EASTMAN INSTITUTE     176
8. GARDEN OF THE SENSES     178
9. SABBATSBERGS KYRKA     180
10. THE ALLEY UNDER ST ERIKSBRON     182
11. THE GRAVE OF POMPE     184
12. STONE OF THE HIGH COUNCIL     186
13. THE KARLBERG RUNESTONE     188
14. ST. MATTEUS PARISH LIBRARY     190
15. BUDO ZEN CENTER     192
16. FÖRENINGEN FÖR FÄKTKONSTENS FRÄMJANDE (FFF)     194
17. MONICA ZETTERLUND PARK     196
18. VILLA BELLONA     198
19. VICTORIAVÄXTHUSET     200
20. WITTROCK TOWER     202
21. CARL ELDH STUDIO MUSEUM     204
22. MESSENGER PIGEON CLUB     206
23. QUEEN CHRISTINA'S GAZEBO     208
24. HAGSTRÖMER MEDICO-HISTORICAL LIBRARY     210
25. TURKISH KIOSK     214
26. CHINESE PAVILION AT HAGA PARK     216
27. CAVE AND PUMP SHAFT AT HAGA PARK     218
28. HAGA CASTLE RUIN     220
29. THE MONTELIUS GRAVE     222
30. HAGALUNDSPARKEN WATER TOWER     224
31. OLLE OLSSON HOUSE MUSEUM     228
32. FILMSTADEN     232

# INSCRIPTION IN
# THE BRUNKEBERGSTUNNELN

*'Tunnel art' in Brunkebergstunneln*

6am-10pm
*Metro: Hötorget or Östermalmstorg*

**O**n the wall of the Brunkeberg walking tunnel (Brunkebergstunneln),
a mysterious, brief message has been hammered into the metal
plates by an unknown scribe. This piece of street art (or should that
be tunnel art?) laconically states: 'My life has a hole the shape of my
15-year-old sister. I miss her every day.' No one seems to know anything
about the message's background.

Aside from this enigmatic text, the Brunkeberg Tunnel is worth a visit on its own merits. The 231-metre-long tunnel between Norrmalm and Östermalm has been featured in many music videos and films.

After 1997 restorations, when the walls were partly covered in shiny metal plates, it became a futuristic location.

It is also slightly dangerous during rush hour, since riding a bicycle in the tunnel is, surprisingly enough in safety-obsessed Sweden, allowed. Pedestrians need to be quick on their feet and alert to the danger of briefcase-toting lawyers and bankers from the surrounding offices riding their bikes at death-defying speeds through the narrow tube. Another danger that causes grumpy old men to shake their umbrellas in anger is the skateboarders that enjoy doing their thing here.

MY LIFE HAS A HOLE
THE SHAPE OF MY 15-YEAR-OLD SISTER.
I MISS HER EVERYDAY.

The tunnel was inaugurated in 1886 by King Oscar II. The building work was troublesome. Luckily, the responsible engineer, Knut Seve Lindmark, finally came up with the ingenious solution of freezing the gravel in the hill to keep it from falling down and hindering the building process. In order to pass through the finished tunnel back in 1886, one had to pay a fee of 2 *öre* (0.02 Swedish crowns). This steep fee was caused by the building project being much more expensive than planned (freezing the side of a hill cost money, especially in the 1880s). However, people turned out to be reluctant to pay this sum, instead opting to climb the steep hill as they had always done. The tunnel was therefore an economic fiasco. Today, passing through it is free and it is more frequently used.

## Unique acoustics

With its peculiar shape and metal-covered rock walls, the tunnel has unique acoustics. The mandolin player Carl, who has been playing tunes there for the last 25 years, gives us proof of this almost daily. He is definitely worth more than 2 öre of your pocket change in appreciation of his stalwart musicianship.

# SWEDENBORG CHURCH

*The first Swedish temple dedicated to the famous mystic*

*Tegnérlunden 7*
*Wednesdays 5pm–7pm*
*On many days, someone will be around during daytime to happily let you in*
*Metro: Odenplan*

Located next to the diminutive park Tegnérlunden, the Swedenborg church, built in the 1920s, belongs to a very special congregation which was once forced to meet in secret. It has many interesting decorations reflecting their singular teaching.

The religious ideas of the mystic Emanuel Swedenborg (1688–1772) (see p. 158) were long forbidden by the stern Church of Sweden. His books had to be printed in other countries, and adherents were not allowed to gather or organise. When Swedish laws on religious dissent became more relaxed, his followers set to work financing and building a church.

At the top of the facade is a red and blue five-point star that can be lit on special occasions. Immediately on the right when you enter the church is an original portrait of Swedenborg which he sat for as an old man – one of few painted from life. At the back wall of the choir, a mural depicts seven angels and a sun. The latter is a 'spiritual sun', a symbol of how God is divine love shining like a sun in heaven.

The three arches behind the altar depict the 'New Jerusalem' mentioned in the Book of Revelation, according to Swedenborg symbolising how the teachings he preached had come down from God in heaven, making the city a representation of his doctrine.

The relief on the left, by sculptor Carl Fagerberg, shows an angel (but with no wings) along with the resurrected Christ and Swedenborg himself. The message is that the teachings came straight from God (even if Swedenborg had regular conversations with angels for almost 30 years). Swedenborg started out as a prominent scientist, and the relief depicts his instrument of science (a square tool – which has led some to speculate on Masonic symbolism, as it is a prominent symbol in such contexts) falling away now that he has received a higher calling.

A recent addition is the spiral candleholder to the left of the entrance, by Nils Sture Jansson. The little golden ball at the origin point of the spiral represents the undivided divine love being disseminated to all of mankind. According to Swedenborg, the spiral was crucial in God's creation of the world, and it is thus the most harmonious shape.

Upstairs is a beautiful research library with many rare, old books and a big wooden model of a flying machine that Swedenborg invented.

The small garden to the right of the entrance has a replica of Swedenborg's Gazebo (see p. 262), the building where he supposedly talked to angels.

For more information about Emanuel Swedenborg, see p. 264.

## Swedenborg's teaching

Swedenborg presented a narrative of Christianity's historical decline, due to loss of the 'inner sense' of scripture and the lives of Christians having become devoid of true spiritual essence. His doctrine has two essential aspects. The first is that there is one God, Jehovah, who incarnated as Jesus to redeem mankind. The second is the obligation to follow the Ten Commandments.

According to Swedenborg, to access the true word of God, the Bible, it must be read with an understanding of the symbolic and hidden spiritual meaning of its texts (with seemingly trivial parts being keys to great mysteries).

The foundation of his theology was laid down in *Arcana Cælestia* (*Heavenly Mysteries*), published in eight Latin volumes from 1749 to 1756. In a significant portion of that work, he interprets the biblical passages of Genesis and Exodus and examines what he says is their inner spiritual sense.

Most of all, Swedenborg was convinced the Bible describes man's transformation from a materialistic to a spiritual being, which he calls rebirth or regeneration. He begins this work by outlining how the creation myth is not an account of the creation of Earth, but an account of man's rebirth or regeneration in six steps represented by the six days of creation. Everything related to mankind in the Bible can ultimately also be related to Jesus Christ and how Christ freed himself from materialistic restrictions through the glorification of his human presence by making it divine.

The *Heavenly Mysteries* rejects the concept of salvation through faith alone (Latin: *sola fide*), since he considered both faith and neighbourly love necessary for salvation, not one without the other, whereas the Reformers taught that faith alone was sufficient, although it had to be a faith which resulted in obedience. In other words, Swedenborg harshly criticised the *sola fide* doctrine of Luther and others.

His entire theory is also based on the principle of correspondences between the spiritual world and the material world – a theory which interested Baudelaire, the French poet: one of his poems is in fact entitled 'Correspondences'. For Swedenborg, the spiritual world and the natural world interpenetrate. Heaven and hell are not rewards or punishments but freely chosen states: heaven is a place of work, altruism and empathy, while hell is the reign of individualism, hatred and distrust, the pursuit of power. The hateful, power-hungry person would leave heaven in fear and return to hell, which suits them better. Mankind is already here and now in the spiritual world, engaged in conversation with those in a spiritual state similar to ours.

In the book *Heaven and Hell*, Swedenborg, who claimed clear-sightedness and the ability to access the spiritual planes (see p. 264), also describes his visits to heaven and hell and reports on the conditions there. In structure, this later book has some similarities to Dante's *Divine Comedy*.

Diverging from the emergent materialism of the time, there is a profound altruism in Swedenborg's thought. Heavenly pleasure, he says, results from the accomplishment of something useful for oneself and for others, while the entire existence of angels consists, in one form or another, of making themselves useful.

Swedenborg further argues that the Trinity was not three persons – the Father, the Son and the Holy Spirit – but one. For him, the Father is the original divine being himself, the Son is the human incarnation of that divine soul (in his terminology, the Divine Human) and the Holy Spirit is the Divine Proceeding (from the Divine Human). He writes that the doctrine of a three-person Trinity arose in the fourth century with the adoption of the Nicene Creed to combat Arianism, but was unknown to the original Apostolic Church.

Although Swedenborg never wanted to set up a Church, on 7 May 1787, The New Church was created in London, following Swedenborg's ideas. It began training ministers and missionaries, who eventually went to the United States, Africa and many other places. Swedenborg believed that the 'African race' was 'in greater enlightenment than others on this earth, since they are such that they think more "interiorly", and so receive truths and acknowledge them'.

# LODGE OF THE KNIGHTS TEMPLAR

*The abstaining knights and their rent-a-lodge*

Kammakargatan 54–56
*Private, but possible to view symbols on gates and look at the information film
constantly shown on a screen in one of the street-level windows (which also
offers a glimpse of the main ritual room)*
*Metro: Odenplan*

Closed to the public, the headquarters of a secret fraternal order, the Knights Templar (Tempel Riddare Orden), stand discreetly on a narrow back street. You can, however, admire the wrought-iron gates bearing the nine-point star symbol of the order.

Its exact meaning appears to be part of the group's inner teachings, and one of their websites states that the star 'contains the Order's knowledge about truth, love, purity and faithfulness' with those 'who devote their time to good being able to perceive in the symbol the refuge it offers'.

Following a typical Masonic structure with initiations through a set number of degrees, there is, however, something different about this order: it is centred around abstaining from alcohol and drugs (ordinary Masonic gatherings, by contrast, usually end with quite boozy dinners). The order's activities otherwise mostly appear to be close to those in the 'ordinary' order of Freemasons, with admission rituals, secret hand grips and passwords, ritualised meals and so on. Judging by the photos in the membership publications available online, the medium age in the order is quite high, even by Masonic standards.

Likely for economic reasons, as it might be difficult to find new teetotal recruits, the order rents its lodge to other groups – in particular, occult groups. Thus, for example, a Rosicrucian–alchemical society, a spiritualist league, and the Ordo Templi Orientis (a magical order based on the teachings of the British occultist Aleister Crowley – who, as a self-described 'drug fiend', was anything but teetotal) all hold gatherings there.

The order originates in a US group, The Templars of Honor and Temperance, which emerged in 1845 from a schism within the older movement Sons of Temperance, allegedly over a lack of elaborate rituals within the latter. The present designation, the Knights Templar, refers to the medieval group of the same name – a martial monastic order created to protect pilgrims in the Holy Land but later accused of heresy and dissolved. However, there is no actual historical link.

Based around 'Christian values', the neo-Templar group is nonetheless non-confessional, and the primary focus is abstaining from intoxication.

No longer active in the US, it still exists across Scandinavia. After arriving there in 1887, the Stockholm Temple was founded in 1899 and now has about 140 members that meet 15 times a year. The 1927–1929 house was constructed specifically for their purposes.

# THE GHOST CASTLE'S COLLECTION

## *A secret art collection*

*Drottninggatan 116*
*The park is open to the public*
*To visit the 'castle' by guided tour only (in Swedish or English) go to:*
*su.se/om-universitetet/kultur-och-historia/konst-vid-stockholms-universitet/*
*visningar*
*Metro: Odenplan*

The so-called 'ghost castle', built around the year 1700, is one of the least-known top-level collections of older art in Sweden, and a supposedly haunted place (see below). Its actual name is the Scheffler Palace, as it was commissioned by the merchant Hans Petter Scheffler.

After passing through several hands, it was donated to Stockholm University in 1924 (back then, the whole neighbourhood was part of its campus, and referred to as Stockholm's Quartier Latin). Today it houses the university's art collection and is used primarily for representation dinners and internal events.

The art includes valuable carpets and furniture along with around 380 works by masters like Pieter Bruegel the younger, Jan Both and Giambattista Tiepolo. There is also a collection of glass products by artists like Simon Gate and Edward Hald, from the Orrefors glassworks. The items on display are mainly used for education and research but are also shown to pre-booked groups.

---

The iron gates of the ghost castle are original, and feature Scheffler's monogram.

---

## The devil, treasures, and ghosts

At the end of the 18th century, a merchant called Jacob von Balthasar Knigge owned the palace. Knigge was an accomplished violinist and a member of the Royal Academy of Music. He was also a severe man, whose cruelty was, according to rumour, so considerable that when he died the Devil collected his soul in a flaming carriage – resulting in a local saying: 'One day the Devil took Knigge'. In and around the palace, strange phenomena started: mirrors and windows broke, mysterious noises, music and song were heard.

Other tales told of subterranean vaults where people had been bricked up together with gold treasures. The notion of secret subterranean spaces may be related to the collapse of a grave in the north end of the palace park in the 1840s, likely the dilapidated final resting place of the original owner, which resulted in the coffin becoming exposed.

The grave was dug up in 1907 and the unidentified remains ended up in the Adolf Fredrik cemetery. The palace park is officially referred to as the 'Ghost Park' and once contained an orangery, a gazebo and other small buildings. Today only the gazebo remains, with its former second floor and luxurious interior removed.

# THE STORYTELLING ROOM

*An otherworldly space for fairy tales*

*Sveavägen 73*
*The room can be visited during the library's opening hours: Monday to Friday*
*10am–8pm, Saturday and Sunday 10am–4pm*
*Metro: Odenplan or Rådmansgatan*

Entering the well-preserved storytelling room at the back of the children's book department in the Stockholm Public Library (inaugurated in 1928) means leaving the mundane world behind. While the dark stairway leading up to the bright main hall of the library symbolises a path to enlightenment by knowledge, the dimly lit storytelling room can be seen as representing the twilight world of fantasy where anything can happen. Its most striking feature is the Post-Impressionist mural of the Sandman by Nils von Dardel (1888–1943) – his only public work.

Portrayed as a pallid boy in green pyjamas and red cap, the Sandman floats in the air, carrying a gigantic umbrella decorated on the inside with a red and yellow painting of St George and the dragon. Under him, an androgynous child lies sleeping on the grass. The latter bears a striking resemblance to the main figure in Dardel's most famous painting, the iconic *Döende dandy* (*Dying Dandy*, 1918), which adds a note of morbidity to the mural.

Around the boy, a host of Lilliputian, fairy-tale figures dance, ride and fight. In the lower-right corner, a king walks arm in arm with a cat. It has been claimed that the king is a portrait of Dardel's father-in-law at the time, the scientist and explorer Axel Klinckowström. Several of the other little figures are also supposedly based on people from the period's high society in Stockholm.

The stucco lustro painting was quite hard work for a middle-aged artist with a heart ailment (not in the least because he had a heavy drinking problem and found it difficult to abstain from the Stockholm nightlife, despite his heart condition). The walls were so cold that they caused him breathing difficulties and pain in the back and breast.

Arriving in Paris after finishing it, he was found to have a 40 degrees Celsius fever and suffered from a pneumonia so serious it almost killed him. This might have influenced the intensity of the mural and the proximity to death somehow present in it: It is arguably reminiscent of traditional deathbed depictions where phantasmagorical figures assail the dying person.

Dardel's public persona was that of a decadent dandy figure, and his bisexuality was well-known. His work was destroyed by the Nazis in Germany as 'degenerate art'. Thus, it seems a bit comical that storytelling sessions in this room featuring drag queens caused enormous outrage a few years ago. Rather, it would seem to be the most logical spot in the entire city for such an event.

When visiting, have a seat on one of the rounded benches, but do not lean against the mural or touch it, as it is quite sensitive.

# ANTHROPOSOPHICAL LIBRARY ⑥

*An esoteric library and course centre*

*Hagagatan 14*
*Monday and Saturday 1.30pm–3.30pm, Wednesdays some weeks, 4pm–6pm*
*Metro: Odenplan*

Anthroposophy is an esoteric teaching founded by the Austrian academic, clairvoyant and utopian thinker Rudolf Steiner (1861–1925) in 1913. On a side street close to the transportation hub Odenplan, you can partake in its mysteries by visiting the Anthroposophical Library.

Entering, you will be struck by the prominent use of pastel colours, and the special design of many objects eschewing sharp corners.

In a prominently placed hand-carved wooden frame next to the bookshelves, in typical anthroposophical design, the intense gaze of Rudolf Steiner meets your eyes.

The purple tablecloths on the reading table are matched by a large chunk of amethyst placed in a niche above it.

The library has been in its present location for a couple of decades and is operated by the Stockholm Circle (whose purpose is to "initiate, conduct, coordinate and support non-profit anthroposophical activities in the Stockholm area"), an economically independent group within the Anthroposophical Society.

The book collection encompasses mostly anthroposophy (such as complete sets of all works by Steiner published in Swedish, for study circle use), but also various other mystical topics.

Several retired anthroposophists work pro bono as librarians, and anyone is welcome to borrow books and join activities. There is also a small antiquarian section, from which you can buy used books in Swedish, German and English.

Down a flight of stairs is a large meeting space with light flowing in from a big skylight and pink walls. It is used for an ambitious programme of lectures, artistic activities, courses and study circles. For example, there are introduction courses to anthroposophy, courses in the Choreocosmos "School of Cosmic and Sacred Dance", music evenings and lunch classes in eurythmy (the performance art developed by Steiner and his collaborators). There are also exhibitions of anthroposophical art.

Anthroposophy has had quite an impact in Sweden, especially through its biodynamic farming and Waldorf schools. But within the teaching, there is also an initiatory path aimed at spiritual development, which is perhaps stressed a bit more at the library than in other places.

For more information about Steiner and anthroposophy, see following double page.

# What is anthroposophy?

Founded by the Austrian occultist Rudolf Steiner (1861–1925), anthroposophy (from the Greek *anthropos* – human – and *sophia* – wisdom) is a spiritual movement that postulates the existence of a spiritual world, accessible to human experience. Steiner also hoped that anthroposophy would help free the individual from any external authority. For Steiner, the human capacity for rational thought would allow individuals to comprehend spiritual research on their own and bypass the danger of dependency on an authority such as himself.

Steiner's spiritual experiences started in childhood, including an encounter at the age of 9 with the spirit of a dead relative. As an adult he became a respected intellectual, wrote a doctoral thesis on the idealist philosopher Johann Gottlieb Fichte (1762–1814) and established himself as an expert on Johann Wolfgang von Goethe (1749–1832).

Many who did not know him well were surprised when he became the leader of the German Theosophical Section. Theosophy was founded in the US in 1875, revolving around the idea that all religions share a secret core, man being able to develop paranormal powers, and complex notions of a cosmic evolution pertaining to the spiritual plane. It drew on old occult ideas and, later, on Indian concepts like reincarnation and karma.

Steiner was critical of the increasing Eastern focus in theosophy. The split became irrevocable when Annie Besant, then president of the Theosophical Society, presented the young boy Jiddu Krishnamurti as the reincarnated Christ.

Steiner strongly objected and considered any comparison between Krishnamurti and Christ to be nonsense; many years later, Krishnamurti also repudiated the assertion. Steiner finally broke free to form the Anthroposophical Society in 1912/1913. There, more emphasis would be placed on Western, Christian symbolism, and he highlighted the Rosicrucian tradition as an important example of this.

Like many other theosophical leaders, Steiner claimed to be clairvoyant, i.e. capable of seeing hidden things. Moreover, he stated he could read the so-called Akashic Chronicles, a kind of library in the spirit world that contains information about everything that has happened and will happen. From this he drew information about the lost civilisations of Lemuria and Atlantis and many other matters. Like Swedenborg (see p. 158) and some spiritualists, Steiner also claimed to have visited other planets through his spirit vision. Steiner further described a path of inner development he felt would let anyone attain comparable spiritual experiences. In his view, spiritual vision could be developed, in part, by practising rigorous forms of ethical and cognitive self-discipline, concentration and meditation. In particular, Steiner believed a person's spiritual development could occur only after a period of moral development.

Steiner was prolific: his collected works comprise some 400 (!) volumes. He spoke of his doctrine as a spiritual science, but at the same time criticised the natural sciences for their materialism. Everyone can learn clairvoyance and spiritual science, he emphasised. Unlike theosophy, his anthroposophy would not include any secret "masters" or selected individuals.

Anthroposophy became successful mainly through its practical focus. It involved biodynamic farming, alternative medicine (today's anthroposophy movement is the owner of the famous Weleda brand) and, of course, the Waldorf schools. In the latter, craftsmanship and artistic expression play an important role.

A special architectural style with a soft, organic look also developed, drawing on influences such as art nouveau/Jugendstil and later expressionism. Today, the main organisation for advocacy of Steiner's ideas, the Anthroposophical Society, is headquartered at the Goetheanum in Dornach, Switzerland, a spectacular example of this architecture.

Anthroposophy influenced several well-known people: painters Piet Mondrian and Wassily Kandinsky, filmmaker Andrei Tarkovsky, child psychiatrist Eva Frommer, to name a few.

© Holger Ellgaard

# THE EASTMAN INSTITUTE

*A striking functionalist interior*

*Dalagatan 11*
*Monday, Wednesday and Thursday 7.30am–5pm, Tuesday 7.30am–6pm,*
*Friday 7.30am–3pm. Weekends closed*
*You can walk in and view most parts of the building during opening hours*
*Metro: Odenplan or St Eriksplan*

Built between 1932 and 1936 and funded by George Eastman (1854–1932) – the American inventor and philanthropist of Kodak photography company fame – the Eastman Institute is a functionalist gem with numerous fun details to marvel at.

Eastman donated one million dollars, a staggering sum at the time, as he wanted to give all Stockholm children the chance to receive treatment for dental problems and ear, nose and throat ailments. This was one of several such donations he made, starting with a dental care centre in Rochester in the US in 1917.

Today the Stockholm Eastman Institute treats children and adults in need of advanced, specialist dental care.

The boxy exterior with its massive marble entrance looks rather grim. The interior is also quite austere, in typical functionalist fashion. However, things are lightened by four fabulous functionalist rocking horses preserved with their original (or at least definitely old) paint intact, complete with beautiful edgewear and patina. Look as well for the big bronze statue of a mother holding a toddler grasping his bite ring.

The former reception booth in wood, glass and chrome has ingeniously been converted into a display for 1930s toys that used to divert kids in the waiting rooms. The toys spin round on a sort of carousel that fits perfectly with the rounded shape of the short end of the booth. Attached to the floor close by is a futuristic 1930s wooden car for kids to ride in.

Some of the spacious, grand rooms have been divided into smaller units. While understandable from a practical point of view, it robs them of their intended grandeur. The architects have at least done their best to retain the original flow of light by using glass doors and top sections of glass for the new walls.

Through the glass door of one meeting room, you can see a big mural depicting *Mors lilla Olle* (*Mother's little Olle*), a boy who meets a bear and feeds him blueberries from his basket in a well-known Swedish children's song by Alice Tegnér from 1895. In the lower right corner is Olle's mother, who cries out in terror and frightens away what her boy took to be a big, friendly dog. On the left side of the same mural is a depiction of Little Red Riding Hood, all in a fine-looking 1930s style.

## A suicide to avoid disability ...

When construction began in 1932, Eastman had shot himself in the heart a few months earlier as he was suffering from a spinal disorder set to make him wheelchair-bound.

# GARDEN OF THE SENSES

*A therapeutic garden*

*Eastmanvägen 29*
*Monday to Thursday 8am–4.30pm, Friday 8am–4pm*
*Metro: Odenpklan or St Eriksplan*

**B**ehind the deafening madness of the playground in Vasaparken lies a small tranquil garden, screened off by a fence and a hedge, that has both botanical and architectural wonders.

Created between 1992 and 1996 by the occupational therapist Yvonne Westerberg (in cooperation with the landscape architect Ulf Nordfjell), it was intended primarily as a tool to treat dementia patients.

This approach, it has been claimed, draws on ideas going all the way back to ancient Greeks like Hippocrates (who supposedly constructed a vast medicinal and therapeutic garden) and the use of cloister gardens in the Middle Ages. Hospital parks and gardens became popular during the 18th and 19th centuries, when it was believed diseases spread via so-called miasma, making walks for fresh air crucial. As healthcare switched to more modern methods such as vaccines, the notion of nature as therapeutic became considered superstition. In recent years, however, it has re-emerged.

Patients suffering from dementia seem to be helped by the stimulation of the senses the garden offers. Under the old chestnut trees, winding bark paths take you past small fruit trees, various herbs, hops, roses, tulips, lilies, clematis, strawberries, blackberries, rhubarb (all depending on the season, of course) and a small pond. One of the most pleasant features is a gazebo from 1784, moved from a different location.

Since many of the patients that spend time here grew up in the traditional agrarian society, some elements of this have also been incorporated, such as a hay rack hung with hay – just like in the days of old. Laundry hanging from a washing line (and a washing board leaned against a tree next to it) is also featured. This is all to recreate childhood memories for the elderly, so they feel at peace and might have their memories jogged. However, the garden is now rarely used by the nearby retirement home, perhaps because Yvonne Westerberg left her job there.

## A place of quietude

Open to everyone, the garden is a perfect spot for quiet contemplation, but of course you should respect the restorative nature of the project and speak in a hushed voice if you go there with others. And turn off that mobile phone.

# SABBATSBERGS KYRKA ⑨

*A peculiar altar in a former inn*

*Eastmansvägen 36*
*svenskakyrkan.se/gustav-vasa-forsamling/sabbatsbergs-kyrka*
*Open for service Tuesdays 11am–noon and for occasional concerts, retreats and other events*
*Metro: St Eriksplan*

The Sabbatsberg hill is unknown territory for most today, and its well-preserved buildings offer an interesting glimpse into Stockholm history. Located on the top of the hill, the Sabbatsberg Church is said to be the city's oldest preserved wooden church. It also has a most peculiar altar area: the pulpit stands right above the altar instead of to its side, as it does in other churches.

It is constructed in this strange manner because the church was originally an inn from 1717, run by a certain Valentin Sabbath (hence the name), and the original architecture required this unconventional solution when remodelling it into a house of God. Why was it then not torn down and replaced with a proper church, you might ask? Well, because it was not a place of worship intended for any ordinary congregation, but for the poorest of the poor. Between 1760 and 1761, all the poorhouses belonging to the city's congregations were relocated here – the idea being to remove them from the central part of the city, so the poor wouldn't cause trouble by begging. Reflecting this, the church has two 18th-century bells mounted on the adjacent Nicolai house. One of them bears an inscription: 'Då detta fattighus åt arma skänker föda, så skänker nåden ljus åt andligt döda' ('When this poorhouse to the destitute gives bread, grace brings light to the spiritually dead').

Connected to the church is a red wooden loft house that may have been used as a dormitory for the inn's guests, which now serves as the sacristy (and on the top floor, with a separate entrance via an outdoor wooden stair, is the studio of an icon painter).

There also used to be a cemetery, with a funeral chapel which was torn down in the 1880s when the Klara gasworks expanded into the neighbourhood. It was replaced with a new chapel and morgue that is today used as office spaces for various creative companies.

Back in the poorhouse days, the presence of a spring with curative properties on the hill meant both the posh and the poor moved about in the area. The rich could buy luxurious pastries and sweets from a bakery, or play nine-pin bowling, while the poor were often severely malnourished. But at least they were given limited access to the health-bringing water itself.

Created in 1734 by the apothecary Johan Julius Salberg, the spring remained in operation until 1968, though most of it had dried up as early as the 1880s.

# THE ALLEY UNDER ST ERIKSBRON

*The shadiest alley in Stockholm, used in several movies, tv-series and music videos*

*Atlasmuren 22*
*The alley is fenced off, but you can get a good view through the fence at any hour of day*
*Metro: St Eriksplan*

Under the main bridge connecting Vasastan and Kungsholmen is a shabby alley unique in the polished, cleaned-up inner city. Because of this, it has been used as a filming site for several movies, TV series and music videos (typically for scenes featuring drug dealing, prostitution and other illicit activities – or as a stand-in for an American urban milieu).

Yet it remains unknown to most people not from the immediate neighbourhood due to its sheltered, concealed location.

For a long time, a completely smashed-up car wreck was parked there, adding to an urban blight aesthetic more 1980s New York than Stockholm.

The alley's walls are covered with graffiti and remnants of street art posters, but hardly any new art has been added since 2015, when the city decided to close the alley off with a fence (the gate in the fencing is, however, quite often left open). Although there was speculation this happened as part of a broader campaign against homeless people setting up camp, it was in fact prompted by fires being lit in the alley – which could have jeopardised the entire bridge by softening the steel beams supporting it.

Moreover, it was a popular site with urban explorers who could potentially have caused some trouble. Specifically, in the inner left corner of the alley, a rotted-away little wooden set of stairs formerly led to a door which opens up to a tunnel containing metro electricity cables (some of which are poorly isolated, and thus quite dangerous). On the right side of the alley, there used to be a record store called Diamond records, which was surely the most hidden shop in the city.

Though you can no longer freely rummage around or attempt mischief in the alley, it is still very much worth a visit to view works by street artists like Akay, Hop Louie and Brat Punisher through the fence (or, if you are lucky, an up-close view if the gate is open).

It is also a symbolic site, being one of the last pockets of tantalising decay. It retains a special atmosphere with the sound of the metro rushing past above, water dripping from the bridge and the dank darkness of the alley frozen in time.

# THE GRAVE OF POMPE

*Final resting place of a loyal and royal dog*

*Karlberg Park*
*Behind Karlberg Castle*
*Open during the park's opening hours (6am–10pm every day)*
*Metro: St Eriksplan, then a 15-minute walk*

Girded with a bronze chain, a small gravestone stands hidden away in Karlberg Park. There are no other graves in the park, so at first sight this might seem peculiar. On closer inspection, it becomes apparent this is indeed no ordinary grave. The inscription on the unassuming stone reads, 'Here King Charles XII's dog Pompe lies buried, in the year 1699'.

As the royal castle Tre Kronor in Old Town burnt down in 1695, Charles (1682–1718) grew up at Karlberg Castle. When Pompe died, Charles was 17 and had been king for two years. Subsequently known as a great warrior king, he was very fond of animals and always took his pet dogs on his military campaigns.

Charles was well-schooled in Latin and classical culture, so the name Pompe may be derived from Pompey (Gnaeus Pompeius Magnus), the famous Roman general. The fact that the king named one of his other dogs Caesar (whom Pompey was a political ally of, though they later became enemies) seems to support this theory.

However, he gave other dogs humorous names like Turk or Snushane (Snuff Male) which might make the alternative interpretation that the name was derived from 'pomp and grandeur' more plausible. Either way, the king sure liked this name, as he would go on to bestow it on two later dogs. Pompe #2 died during a campaign in Poland in 1703 and #3 under similar circumstances in Hungary in 1714, meaning neither were buried in Stockholm.

The grave site is often decorated with flowers and sometimes more unexpected things – such as Wunderbaums hung on the girding. It has also been defaced a couple of times, likely due to everything connected to Charles XII being somewhat controversial because of his popularity with neo-Nazis who regard him as a symbol of Sweden as a warrior nation.

However, he was also a quite multicultural monarch in many ways who (probably) introduced various Turkish dishes in Sweden after his travels there, spoke nine languages (with a varying degree of proficiency), and for the first time in the country's history granted Jews and Muslims the right to settle and practice their religion.

## A poem for a dog

There is even a contemporary poem praising Pompe, by Israel Holmström (1661–1708), recounting how the dog slept in the king's bed every night and then died at his feet, weary from age and travels – and then proclaiming that many a proud and fair maiden would wish to live as Pompe did (sleeping in the king's bed, that is) while a thousand heroes yearn to die as he did.

# STONE OF THE HIGH COUNCIL 

*A cryptic marker of military traditions*

*Karlberg Park*
*Behind Karlberg Castle*
*Can be visited during the park's opening hours (6am–10pm)*
*Metro: St Eriksplan, then a 15-minute walk*

Behind Karlberg Castle, a huge rock tucked away among the trees of Karlberg Park has a puzzling ornament attached to it – a gigantic iron monocle, complete with chain.

It looks as if the rock itself is a huge eye, or a giant has walked past and dropped his monocle. The inscription on the monocle is quite mysterious to the casual passer-by, stating simply, 'The High Council 1896–1996'. Nothing more, and no explanation of what this council governs.

The mysterious High Council is, however, not some shady Illuminati group having left a tantalising clue to their activities, but the council of cadettes at nearby Karlberg Military Academy.

As the oldest educational institution of its kind in the world (that remains in its original buildings, and on the original site of foundation), the academy has more than a few archaic traditions – including a peculiar internal language (Carlbergiana) in the council, made up of 19th-century Stockholm slang and military lingo. Carlbergiana also has its own peculiar way of spelling ordinary words.

The council is ruled by The Four Powerful, who are elected democratically by the students, and its highest leader is The Most Powerful Man (or woman, now), who also carries a special sword used in rituals.

There are also various other functionaries within the council, such as a castle poet and a mead-giver (the latter being responsible for student pubs). Once founded due to students being displeased with their education, the council is a central part of the activities on campus. Today it organises balls and the more sinister sounding 'Viking Blot' – a blot historically signifying a bloody sacrifice to the Norse gods, but here most likely something a bit less violent.

In typical Swedish spirit, there is also work being done to increase the number of female cadettes. Another ritual is 'The Baptism of Cadette Pihlqvist', a mythological enactment involving figures like a pastor, mourners and dancing angels. There is also supposedly a secretive 'Ceremony of Light', the details of which are unknown even to most of the 200 cadettes educated each year, and certainly to all outsiders.

# THE KARLBERG RUNESTONE

(13)

*A serpent-adorned Viking-age remnant*

Behind Karlberg Castle
Can be visited during the park's opening hours (6am–10pm)
Metro: St Eriksplan, then a 15-minute walk

In Stockholm's inner (well, more or less) city there is only one free-standing runestone, but it was very nearly turned into rubble or buried permanently in the 1920s.

Back in those days, a pastoral area close to today's Karlberg Park was popular with local kids playing football. A group of boys were hanging out there in the summer of 1922. As it was quite warm, they put their sandwiches under a large, flat stone that had ended up there during roadworks. The stone would also be good to get some shade from the sun, one of them figured. When he stuck his head into the cavity under it, he spotted carved runes. One of the boys had an elder brother who helped copy the runes. He then showed them to his teacher at school, who was able to read them. The Swedish National Heritage Board was informed, and the stone was transported (on a wheelbarrow!) to the grounds of the nearby Karlberg Castle, where it was put in its present location.

Today, the carving has been filled in with red paint, but this was not the case back when it was made.

The runes are quite sparse, simply saying, 'Anund and Torgils had the stone raised in remembrance of Åsgöt'.

The ornamentation is more interesting and evocative than the text, featuring a Christian cross with a winding, serpentine dragon curled around it – on whose body the runes are carved.

The dragon may be the fearful Nidhögg, the creature gnawing away at the roots of the world tree Yggdrasil in ancient Norse myth. The cross it is coiled around can thus also be seen as Yggdrasil, even though the stone dates from the period after Sweden became Christian. The top one of its eight arms divides into two, making for a total of nine – equivalent to the nine worlds located along the trunk of Yggdrasil. The fact that the dragon seems to be biting its own tail may also point to a possible identification with Jörmungandr, the gigantic serpent offspring of the god Loki and the giantess Angerboda that lies coiled around all of Middle-earth. It was connected to the chaos powers that the gods of order were to confront at the apocalyptic Ragnarök, where Thor slays Jörmungandr but then only manages to walk nine paces before he falls dead to the ground – poisoned by the bites of the serpent. After the spread of Christianity, Jörmungandr became connected with the biblical sea monster Leviathan, a creature subsequent magical systems would list as one of the four crown princes of hell.

# ST MATTEUS PARISH LIBRARY  ⑭

*A time-warp library with a collection of rare
detective novels*

Västmannagatan 92, second floor
Monday, Tuesday and Thursday 2pm–7pm, Wednesday 10am–3pm, Friday
10am–1pm
Metro: Odenplan

The library run by the St Matteus parish – discreetly located on the second floor of an old building – has changed little since it moved there in 1916. The staff will even write out your library card on an old typewriter! Its collection includes a large portion of detective novels, both recently published and old, rare volumes. This might seem an atypical focus for a church-run library, but it is due to one of the former vicars having been a passionate fan of the genre.

The library is open to anyone, not just those living in the area or members of the Church of Sweden. The interior is stunning, with well-worn, creaky wooden floors and cherrywood bookshelves lined up along the turquoise-green walls. Behind the counter are further rooms, filled with high shelves stuffed with books. A room on the right offers cosy sofas and armchairs along with a huge table for study circles and discussion groups. It is all lit by handsome, old lamps.

## 'We have plenty of time, just for you'

While there are whole sections of beautiful, old volumes, the librarians keep the selection very up to date with constant acquisitions. In another sense, however, time moves deliberately slow here, as the stated motto of the librarians is 'We have plenty of time, just for you'. When you enter, leave the rush and cold effectiveness of the outside world behind! Instead of scanning your loans, the librarian uses a proper, old-school stamp.

## The education of an originally proletarian neighborhood

The intention of the library was never to preach Christianity, but to further the literary education of the originally proletarian neighbourhood (built as living quarters for the workers in the Rörstrand porcelain factory). This is a concept typically associated with the 'people's libraries' created by the state in the 1930s, but the church anticipated such endeavours years before. However, this entailed special rules for borrowing books: For every volume of light entertainment, you also had to bring home two volumes of high-brow literature (this is no longer the case, though)! With the rise of the state-run libraries, most parish libraries were closed, but St Matteus remained, to the great joy of book lovers and retrophiles. You are welcome to browse the selection of books on your own, ask the knowledgeable librarians for recommendations, or just sink down in one of the armchairs and read (even one of your own books or newspapers).

# BUDO ZEN CENTER

## 15

*A slice of Japan in Sweden*

*Hagagatan 39*
*Check the club's website (iogkf.se) for training times and contact them in advance to visit as a spectator. New students are accepted at the start of every term*
*Metro: Odenplan*

Visiting the Budo Zen Center is like stepping into a temple in Kyoto.

Created by Swedish karate legend Björn Jonzon (born 1950) in 1984, this dōjō greets visitors with a big portrait of Chōjun Miyagi – the founder of the dōjō's style of karate. It is probably the most aesthetically appealing martial arts club in Sweden, and unique in terms of artistic value even in a broader context.

After the entrance, you pass an antechamber and cross a small curved wooden bridge, flanked by a big bonsai tree, and enter the main hall through a pair of traditional shōji (wood and translucent paper) doors.

Along one of the walls is a carefully recreated facade of a traditional Japanese house, elevated above the floor and with a wooden platform running along it. Hung on its walls are weapons like sai, bokken, tonfa and nunchaku. You would be excused for thinking you have entered a movie set for a samurai film.

The romantic setting is home to one of the most traditional karate clubs in Sweden, which retains close links to instructors in Okinawa (karate's place of origin). The name of the type of karate practised is Gōjū-ryū, meaning 'hard-soft style' in Japanese.

Sensei Björn Jonzon started training Japanese martial arts in the 1960s and has been running a dōjō since 1975. In 1981 in Okinawa he met his mentor, Morio Higaonna, and in 1983 acquired the lease on an abandoned welding workshop where he started building his own karate centre. He did most of the construction work by himself, and the dōjō is constantly changing, with little improvements added over time. Today, the Stockholm club has around 100 members and subsections in three other places in Sweden.

Crossing a second little bridge back into the antechamber, a temple-style double door sealed off with a cord opens into a space for meditation. This serene room contains an atmospherically lit stone Buddha and is lined with a platform provided with cushions.

Sensei Björn also has a background in Zen training with the well-known American Sanbō Kyōdan Zen teacher Philip Kapleau, who emphasised the adaptation of meditation techniques to local cultural conditions. The dōjō thus offers a space for physical and mental–spiritual development, firmly grounded in Japanese tradition but adjusted to Swedish circumstances.

# FÖRENINGEN FÖR FÄKTKONSTENS FRÄMJANDE (FFF)

## 16

*Stockholm's oldest fencing club*

*Döbelnsgatan 60*
*You can view fencing classes through the big glass windows. If you ask the*
*fencers politely, you may be allowed to sit in on a class to view training up close*
*Metro: Rådmansgatan*

With its spacious fencing hall located on a back street, Föreningen för Fäktkonstens Främjande (FFF, The League for the Furthering of Fencing) offers a glimpse into the old traditions and modern sportsmanship of competition fencing. The two primary weapons used at the club are épée and sabre, but to a lesser extent foil is also taught.

Founded in 1901, FFF is the oldest Swedish fencing club still in existence and one of the most successful in international competitions.

Its first fencing master (Maître d'Armes) was a Frenchman, Eugène Fillol, who from 1901 to 1914 was crucial to the consolidation of the club and the development of modern competition fencing in Sweden. FFF continued recruiting foreign fencing masters to get the best instructors available globally, among them well-known fencers like the Italian Francesco Gargano in the 1930s and the German Rudolf Meckel in the 1960s. In the 1990s, FFF became the first Swedish club to employ a female fencing coach, Ulrika Larsson.

Today, the club offers both elite and amateur training. It also hosts fencing events for company kick-offs, stag and hen parties, and children's birthday parties. It has 350 active members, aged from 9 to 85. Royalty like Prince Gustaf Adolf (the father of our present king, and a successful competition fencer) and his daughter Princess Brigitta have been among the FFF fencers. Counting several world championship winners among its members through its more than 120-year history, FFF fencer Johan Harmenberg also won an Olympic gold medal in 1980.

The club has been in its present 580-square-metre location since 2011, and the fencing hall has 12 pistes, two changing rooms, a workshop for sword repairs and a smaller, aquarium-like room facing the street. The latter room is typically used for one-on-one fencing lessons or smaller groups and offers passing spectators a prime view of the goings-on. Attached to the wall is an arm holding an épée that fencers can hone their skills against when no instructor or other pupil is available. On the left short end, you can see old oil paintings of former fencing masters in the club – moustache-adorned and stern-looking.

# MONICA ZETTERLUND PARK

*A singing bench and hidden faces*

*Roslagsgatan 20*
*Metro: Rådmansgatan*

There are a couple of little surprises in store at the park that bears the name of celebrated Swedish jazz singer and actress Monica Zetterlund (1937–2005).

Firstly, when you approach the prominently placed curved teak bench to sit down, hidden speakers begin playing her songs. The repertoire encompasses 17 compositions, enough for around an hour of enjoyment (she recorded some 700 albums, so this is a very small slice of her total work!).

Secondly, you should turn your gaze toward the lamp posts, as Zetterlund's profile has subtly been incorporated into them (most clearly visible against a light sky) – something you will only notice if looking specifically for it.

The initially nameless park was created in the early 1980s, when the adjacent inn Clas på hörnet (see p. 61) was renovated. It was named after Zetterlund the year after her death, based on a so-called 'citizen suggestion'. By 2010, the Monica Zetterlund Society had managed to raise 300,000 Swedish crowns from hundreds of donors, which paid for the bench and the lamp posts.

The bench was designed by the artist Fredrik Wretman and has a high, curved back shutting out the street noise and making the park a perfect spot for a relaxing break from the surrounding hustle and bustle. Over time, the teak has taken on a beautifully weathered, silvery colour.

When Wretman was approached, he immediately explained he did not want to make just another bronze statue, but a sound work instead – Zetterlund was, after all, famous primarily for her voice!

The park has a small lawn, and an impressive number of different plants, including magnolias, lady's mantle, daylilies and plantain lilies. It also contains a tiny playground with a minuscule sandbox.

Zetterlund lived close by on Birger Jarlsgatan 117, and died in a fire started by her smoking in bed. As she was wheelchair-bound, she was unable to make it out of her apartment.

## Zetterlund's hairdresser

Right across from the park is the hairdresser G. Azar, who used to cut Zetterlund's hair. Mr Azar's salon is a bit of a time capsule, with old barber chairs and 1970s decorations, and he has quite a few stories to tell about the singer while he cuts hair (payment by cash only, which is very odd and old-school for Stockholm!).

# VILLA BELLONA

## 18

## *The last remaining Arts and Crafts 'professor house'*

*Universitetsvägen 8*
*If you ask nicely, it might be possible to enter the house during office hours*
*Metro: Universitetet, then a 5-minute walk*

A remarkable example of Arts and Crafts-inspired architecture, Villa Bellona was one of seven so-called professor villas built in 1907 for academics working at the Royal Academy of Agriculture. When the present grim-looking modern campus for Stockholm University was built between 1961 and 1971, the other six villas were torn down. Villa Bellona was temporarily spared to function as the office for the building staff, but it ended up becoming permanently preserved. Dwarfed by the

stern, colossal modernist university buildings, it stands as a reminder of very different architectural ideals from a bygone age.

Villa Bellona was designed by architect Lars Johan Lehming (1871–1940), who travelled extensively in Sweden, England, Germany and Italy to study old local building craft. Lehming designed several private residences around Stockholm, as well as doing work for the Swedish army. He was fired from the latter post, however, after designing a peace monument at the Swedish–Norwegian border in Morokulien in 1914.

For the professor villas project, Lehming was heavily influenced by the British Arts and Crafts Movement. Originating in 1850s England, and reaching its apex from the 1880s to the 1910s, it was a type of hyper-aesthetic, anti-industrial current, often with a socialist underpinning, that emphasised traditional craftsmanship. Drawing on Gothic Revival architecture, folk architecture and romantic notions about the rustic and genuine Middle Ages, its representatives simultaneously rejected purely historicising styles and underscored the importance of creating something new, modern and functional while honouring (primarily medieval) tradition.

Villa Bellona was one of the smallest of the seven villas, which were all red-painted wooden constructions resting on massive stone foundations. There are many beautiful details to discover when looking at the building's exterior. For example, check out the huge door hinges in black-painted hammered iron that would look at home in William Morris' 1859 Red House in Bexleyheath, England.

Also impressive are the shingled top part of its walls and an enormous window section following the shape of the interior staircase. Today, Villa Bellona is home to the Stockholm University Innovation office.

## 19

# VICTORIAVÄXTHUSET

*Unearthly giant waterlilies*

*Veit Wittrocks väg 11*
*Weekdays 11am–4pm and weekends 11am–5pm, May to September*
*Metro: Universitetet, then a 15-minute walk*

Inaugurated in 1900, Victoriaväxhuset (The Victoria Hothouse) is in extravagant, turn-of-the-century style, with a glass cupola and supporting structures in cast iron. Following a plan from the firm Schmidt & Schlieder in Leipzig, it was built in 1899 and created a considerable buzz. Today, the hothouse is more of a forgotten and hidden pearl.

It was built primarily to cultivate and display the water lily *Victoria amazonica*, hence its name. This, however, is not the only attraction for the botanically inclined. The greenhouse also offers lotus, mangrove and papyrus, among other plants.

With a temperature upwards of 30 degrees Celsius and a humidity level of around 80 per cent, a visit to the greenhouse is like a quick trip to the tropics. The humidity also entails heavy wear on the cast-iron structure, which has had to undergo extensive renovations.

The central pond is filled with the spectacular, colossal water lilies, the world's biggest species, whose leaves are sturdy enough to carry a weight up to 100 kilos (if evenly distributed). When in bloom, once a year (around 24–27 June), the flowers open up after dark. Each flower remains open for two nights. The first night, it is white, turning pink the second, with an appealing smell similar to pineapple. Pollinated by nocturnal beetles and other insects active by night, the flower closes around its visitors in the morning and traps them until the next night so they have ample time to perform their task. Once pollinated, the flower is retracted below the water surface.

There is a distinctly unearthly quality to the scale of the Victoria, and the leaves (which are up to 3 metres in diameter) have the appearance of something from a different planet.

# WITTROCK TOWER

## *The eccentric professor's folly*

*Gustafsborgsvägen 18*
*bergianska.se*
*You can climb the stairs to the tower at all times of day and peek in. The interior is only open to the public during organised walks in the area a few times during the year. Check the website for more info*
*Metro: Universitetet, then a 15-minute walk*

At the time when the Bergianska botanical garden moved from Karlberg to Frescati in the late 19th century, its head was a certain Professor Veit Wittrock (1839–1914). He was highly eccentric and, for example, wore a heavy fur coat throughout the year – even in the warmest summer months.

Wittrock became controversial with his project *Fjällen*, a sort of miniature version in the botanical garden of the mountains in northern Sweden. Today, alpine and mountain plants from different parts of the world are still displayed there on top of small artificial hills. This turned out to be less than popular with the public, who preferred more spectacular and exotic things, such as tropical plants.

In 1908, Professor Wittrock commissioned the architect Oskar Lindberg to design a tower on a hill above the shore of Brunnsviken. It was primarily employed to store the professor's collection of seeds and cones, but he also used it as his office. He delighted in inviting visitors to take in the breathtaking view. As it was built during the height of nationalist fervour in Sweden, the tower was originally painted in the same blue colour as the Swedish flag, with yellow details just like the cross on the flag.

When it was renovated eight years later, a viewing platform was added to the roof, originally intended to be crowned by a huge metal pine cone (which ended up becoming just a plain metal ball).

For a long time, horse races on the ice of Brunnsviken were a popular spectacle during cold winters. The judges of these races used the tower to get a clear view of events on the ice. This was necessary, as the races were often won by very small margins. The horses ran around a circular course, with a military band playing in the middle. In 1927, the Solvalla racetrack opened, and horse racing enthusiasts now had a permanent arena for their sport. When the ice did not freeze properly during the winter of 1930, it meant the end for the Brunnsviken horse races.

In spite of its practical functions as a viewpoint for judges and home to the botanical collections, the tower could also be seen as a folly in the vein of the whimsical buildings built by Gustav III on the other side of the water – but in this case with a peculiar professor as the instigator.

Today, the tower houses artists' studios, and you can glimpse jars with brushes and works of art in progress through the windows. The interior remains more or less unchanged since the 1930s.

# CARL ELDH STUDIO MUSEUM

*An artist's studio frozen in time*

*Lögebodavägen 10*
*Tuesday to Sunday noon–4pm in June, July and August*
*April and October, Saturday to Sunday noon–4pm*
*May and September, Thursday to Sunday noon–4pm*
*Metro: Tekniska Högskolan, then a 15-minute walk*

The first thing that will strike you when approaching the Carl Eldh Studio Museum is the lovely smell of tar. All the walls of the building, perched on a cliff in Bellevue Park, are tarred – a traditional treatment of wood that repels water. Constructed as a studio for the sculptor Carl Eldh (1873–1954) between 1918 and 1919, the structure is architecturally modern but built with old-fashioned materials.

Eldh was one of Sweden's most famous sculptors back in his day but had been forced to move around quite a bit to find places that met his studio demands. To get the right amount of light, he had for example rented former shops with big windows. His friend, the architect Ragnar Östberg (1866–1945), designed this permanent studio after a suitable plot of land had been found, in what was than a remote part of the city.

Entering the museum, Eldh's personality is still evident in the ascetic panelling and rough floors. On display are many of his sculptures in varying scales, sometimes making you feel like a little ant and sometimes like Gulliver in the land of the Lilliputians, making for a dizzying demonstration of Eldh's tremendous talent and skill. The huge window sections, designed to maximise working hours, provide beautiful natural light – so beautiful that even visitors may look like sculptures wrought by the master's hand. Everything remains as it was when the artist passed: sculpting tools, some personal belongings, plaster and clay sketches, and a handful of stone and bronze pieces.

After Eldh's death in 1954, his daughter Elsa made a spartan permanent home for herself in the building and, in 1963, opened it as a museum for the public that she ran on her own. An enthusiastic gardener, her green fingers mean the garden still has an abundance of snowdrops, crocuses, tulips, narcissus, lilacs, rhododendrons, roses, peonies, lavender, irises, hostas, rhubarb, chives, marguerites and great masterwort. When Elsa became too old to run the museum, it closed. However, only a few years later, it was reopened by a private foundation.

# MESSENGER PIGEON CLUB

*Very special birds*

Bellevueparken
*The club itself is not open to visitors*
*Metro: Rådamansgatan or Tekniska Högskolan*

On top of the hill in the Bellevue park, a stone's throw from the old city limit, is a delightfully archaic messenger pigeon club where the birds are trained to fly long distances and return to a specific location. Such activities have been going on there since 1911.

The small wooden house is home to 700 messenger pigeons, trained by Saheb and Jamahl from Baghdad. Saheb arrived in Sweden from war-torn Iraq in 1984, and had been a pigeon trainer back home as well – though the activities were, as one would expect, no longer possible when full-scale war broke out and bombs were dropping.

In Sweden, the threat is of a different nature. Perched atop the Wenner-gren high-rise close by, a northern goshawk waits for any opportunity to catch pigeons. It has often been successful in its hunting, and many pigeons have been lost that way. The northern goshawk can often be seen quite clearly if you take a pair of binoculars.

Messenger pigeons have been used in many wars, including during both world wars – where they sometimes made important contributions when other means of communication were impossible. During World War II, 32 American pigeons were even decorated with medals. The Swedish Army used messenger pigeons until the 1950s, and in a couple

of European countries they are reportedly still in use (there is no need to worry about electronic interception or hacking when using pigeons, which might be an advantage now).

Competitions with messenger pigeons are popular in many places in Europe, and the first prize in certain events abroad can be up to 100,000 Swedish crowns. In Sweden, the national organisation for messenger pigeon trainers has 500 members.

The messenger pigeon club's location – with the combination of a busy motorway right below the hill and the idyllic setting with several 18th-century wood houses – makes for an interesting contrast between old and new, tranquillity and stress.

The interior of the building is not open to the public, but you can marvel at the beautifully weathered, hand-painted old sign announcing the premises belong to the Stockholm messenger pigeon club. And if you feel up to witnessing the brutality of nature, you can perhaps catch sight of a northern goshawk attack!

---

In Brussels, there is a sculpture in honour of messenger pigeons and, in Barcelona, there is a pigeon club open to the public. See, from the same publisher, the books *Secret Brussels* and *Secret Barcelona*.

---

## *Origin of the racing pigeon's amazing capacity*

Whether released at 500 m or 100 km from home, even in certain cases over 1,000 km, the messenger pigeon has a fantastic ability to always know its way back. The reason for these exceptional skills is still unknown, but some people attribute the gift to the presence of tiny crystals in the brain. This trait was detected a long time ago, notably by Julius Caesar who, during the invasion of Gaul, used homing pigeons to send messages back to Rome to inform headquarters of his campaign's progress. On the other hand, so there's no misunderstanding, the pigeon you sometimes see in films, which is released and asked to take a message somewhere and then return, doesn't exist. The pigeon is only (so to speak) capable of returning home. This is why, in order to send a message to several places, pigeons raised at each destination have to be used. To send several successive messages to the same place, the corresponding number of pigeons have to be taken out. There's nothing miraculous in the voyage, but it would be difficult to receive messages with the pigeons moving from dovecote to dovecote.

# QUEEN CHRISTINA'S GAZEBO

*Tiny, well-preserved baroque pavilion*

*Annerovägen 4*
*Only open upon prior booking for a private dinner – a truly special* chambre
séparée
*Website: stallmastaregarden.se/moten/vara-lokaler/kristinapaviljongen*
*Metro: Odenplan*

Situated on the premises of the inn Stallmästargården, Queen Christina's gazebo is a magical place where you get the feeling of time having stood still. Entering Haga Park from Vasastan, it stands immediately on your right-hand side. This tiny, well-preserved structure, with a beautifully painted ceiling, has roots stretching back to the 17th century.

However, in spite of its name, the connection to Queen Christina is rather tenuous. In the 1630s, one of the illegitimate sons of King Charles IX bestowed lifelong use of land and a building (located where the gazebo now stands) to his much-appreciated equerry (master of stables). In the year 1645, the headstrong and somewhat eccentric Queen Christina – who often hunted and rode in the area – was taken with the site, which faces the attractive shore of Brunnsviken. She decided to celebrate midsummer there. When word of this royal infatuation with the equerry's plot of land spread, the stable master soon decided to make money from it and opened an inn.

By the 1730s, the inn was run by an industrious royal falconer, Lucas Boogers. He had a glassed-in octagonal gazebo, built in the previous century, moved there from the inner city. According to one source, it was also Boogers who planted four small-leaved linden trees in front of it (today, only two remain). The gazebo stands on the spot where the building in which Queen Christina celebrated midsummer used to be. This, then, is the only connection to her.

## The many Queen Christina sites

There are, in fact, numerous buildings and places in Sweden that have been named after the fabled queen, who is the subject of so many tall tales. There also seems to be a special connection between her and linden trees, as there are two trees planted on the grounds of castles in Uppland named after her (though one or both of them may in fact have been planted by – and named after – her grandmother, who bore the same name). The name usually employed in reference to this specific site in Hagaparken is 'Queen Christina's arbour', with the linden trees forming one side of the arbour, and the little pavilion the other.

# HAGSTRÖMER
# MEDICO-HISTORICAL LIBRARY

*An extremely atmospheric and little-known library*

*Annerovägen 12*
*It is possible to book guided tours of the library (via hagstromerlibrary@ki.se)*
*or to visit the reading room*
*Wednesday and Thursday, 9am–noon*
*Metro: Odenplan, then a 20-minute walk*

Right next to a busy motorway lies a former courthouse, built between 1905 and 1907, adorned with Jugendstil owls. The court moved out in 1980, and it was then rented out as offices to various private companies. Today, however, it is the little-known home of the atmospheric Hagströmer Medico-Historical Library (Hagströmerbiblioteke).

Since 1997 this library has gathered collections of manuscripts and more than 100,000 rare, old books from the world-renowned research hospital Karolinska Institutet (founded in 1810), the Swedish Society of Medicine (founded in 1807) and the *Collegium Medicum* (in operation 1663–1812).

Many of the books are extremely scarce and valuable first editions. Among them are the physicist and chemist Carl Benedicks' (1875–1958) collection of books on alchemy and older chemistry. The stomach-churning Wessler collection focuses on dentistry and, alongside books and some gruesome objects, also contains a large collection of related prints. Other highlights in the library include a first edition of Linnaeus' groundbreaking biological work *Systema Naturae* (1735).

The Hagströmer Library was located on the hospital grounds where the new Aula Medica now stands before moving to its very charming new home.

At the centre of the building is the big former courtroom, which now has beautiful green bookcases along all walls and display cases in the middle. Though many of the original details were torn out in previous decades, the historical ambiance has been restored to a great extent.

The library irregularly hosts lectures and exhibitions, often striking bridges between the arts, the medical sciences and the humanities in interesting ways. It also offers a residential research fellowship for scholars wanting to work with the collections.

## A giant's cauldron

The building has a very peculiar secret in its basement: a 3-metre-deep so-called "giant's cauldron". It is a cylindrical pothole once drilled in the solid rock under a prehistoric glacier by meltwater streams grinding rocks against it. Discovered when preparing the ground for the building back in 1905, it was left as an underground curiosity. Sometimes it fills with subterranean water almost to the brim, while at other times it is almost completely dry. It can be viewed by visitors as part of guided tours.

# TURKISH KIOSK

*An exotic pavilion that was once the site of secret meetings*

*Haga Park*
*The building is not open to the public but can be viewed from the outside – you can peer in through the windows to see the interior*

Hidden in the foliage on a hill off the beaten paths in Haga Park, directly opposite the Chinese Pavilion, the Turkish Kiosk is a true, secret delight.

The kiosk can be accessed via a small footpath, and you can peer in through the windows to see the interior. It has a hexagonal main chamber, with three antechambers (all containing a gold and white ceramic tile stove) in different directions that function as entrances. The roof is shaped like a (Turkish) tent, and crowned by a Turkish Islamic half-moon. Seldom used and not open to the public, its design reflects the orientalism of times past.

Kiosk is a Turkish term (*köşk*) of Persian origin, meaning pavilion or gazebo – and this little structure in the park has never been a kiosk in the sense that refreshments, newspapers or the like have been sold there. At the time it was built (1786–1788), 'kiosk' still held its Turkish meaning of a small pavilion, specifically a construction that was open on one or several sides to offer a fine view. Today, some of the view is obscured by trees that have grown tall during the last two centuries, but much of the original sight line is kept free.

Like the majority of the hidden highlights of Haga Park, and the more obvious ones, the kiosk was commissioned by King Gustav III. This was in fact the first new structure erected by him in the park. The architect was Fredrik Magnus Piper (this being the only one of his numerous suggestions that was actually built, and only after several versions of it had been scrutinised by the fault-finding, picky king). The powder blue and white interior (inspired by Pompeii) was designed by Louis Masreliez.

On New Year's Eve 1788, the kiosk was inaugurated with a 'Turkish' birthday party for Gustav III's brother, Duke Charles (later Charles XI-II), who was deeply engaged in Freemasonry and ritual magic. The next New Year's Eve, a play by the famed Carl Michael Bellman (1740–1795) featuring actors from the Royal Dramatic Theatre premiered there.

But not all was frivolity in the kiosk: Occasionally, King Gustav III would use it to gather his closest associates, most of whom were Freemasons like himself and his brother, to hold clandestine council. For example, this was where the war against Russia 1788–1790 was planned – the war that would contribute to the frustration among Swedish noblemen that ended with the assassination of King Gustav in 1792.

© Holger.Ellgaard

# CHINESE PAVILION
# AT HAGA PARK

## *A manifestation of monarchist ideals?*

*The pavilion can be visited between 11am and 5pm – at all other hours the gates below it are closed, as it is surrounded by private properties*
*Metro: Odenplan*

© Frankie Fouganthin

Tucked away on a leafy hill to the side of the main walking trail in Haga Park, the Chinese Pavilion is a colourful folly that may hold a shrouded anti-democratic symbolism.

Commissioned from the architect and artist Louis Jean Desprez (1743–1804) in 1788, the pavilion is octagonal and open to all sides. Its wooden pillars, painted in bright colours, support a slanted tin roof adorned with dragons. In the middle of the pavilion, there once stood a large octagonal table echoing the shape of the pavilion itself. Surrounding the structure, there were pedestals borne by Chinese figurines. All that is long gone, but the bases of the pedestals can still be discerned.

The pavilion has been renovated several times, and in 1974 the wooden dragons adorning the roof were substituted with new ones made from glass fibre. The bells that used to hang from the dragons, jingling in the wind, have been removed.

When King Gustav III, the monarch responsible for the creation of Haga Park, was a boy, his father gave his mother a grandiose, Chinese-inspired pavilion as a birthday gift. It was little Gustav, dressed as a Chinese prince, who handed the golden key to the pavilion to his mother. This was the beginning of a life-long fascination with China for him.

The endeavours of the Swedish East India Trading Company (founded in 1731) made Chinese culture popular in Sweden. Tea drinking, collecting Chinese antiques, and imitations of Chinese architecture all became the highest fashion. But the influence was not merely aesthetic. King Gustav III and his circle of advisors were impressed with how the supposedly harmonious model country China was governed by a powerful monarch surrounded by his 'Mandarins' – highly educated bureaucrats.

The diplomat and politician Carl Fredrik Scheffer (1715–1786), Grand Master of the Swedish Order of Freemasons between 1753 and 1774, and an important mentor for King Gustav III, argued that the latter's 1772 *coup d'état* (where he established an absolute monarchy, and crushed the power of the *Riksdag* of the Estates) was in fact a reversion to the same ideal system of governance that characterised China. Against this background, the pavilion can be seen as a manifestation of monarchist ideals, rather than just an amusing folly.

# CAVE AND PUMP SHAFT AT HAGA PARK

*Traces of a fanciful project*

The cave and the pump shaft on top of the mountain are open all day
Metro: Odenplan, then a 25-minute walk

A long the main path in Haga Park, a cave opens into the mountainside. What most do not know is that this is a man-made cave, and part of an elaborate plan to construct an artificial waterfall that was never realised. If you climb to the top of the mountain, the remains of the pump shaft can be seen.

During his travels in France and Italy in 1783–84, King Gustav III was dazzled by the ingenious cascades and fountains in various gardens and parks. Naturally, he wanted something similar for his own park in Stockholm.

The idea was to create a small lake on top of the mountain, with a pump station to draw water from the natural lake below. The pump would be concealed within a building in medieval pseudo-Gothic style.

Plans shifted back and forth, and later an obelisk was to be erected atop the mountain. There was also talk of an observation tower in the form of a high column where the base was decorated with sculpted horses and topped with a statue of King Gustav Vasa. All this was quite typical of the fanciful ideas entertained by Gustav III.

In 1786, blasting was initiated for the shaft through the mountain to draw water. This turned out to be costly and slow work. As steam power was all the rage, this was probably intended to power the pump. A while later, however, it was decided to instead use a windmill for this purpose. A windmill was acquired from Kalmar in south-eastern Sweden – but it mysteriously disappeared on its way to Stockholm.

After King Gustav was assassinated in 1792, work on the project, like many others, stopped almost immediately.

Many big rocks have been hewn down on the cave floor, possibly by workers frustrated with all their efforts being for nothing. The tun-

nel reaches 16 metres into the mountain, and the daring can climb down into it. Be careful, as the surface is slippery. And remember to take a proper flashlight.

After the level was lowered in 1863, water was no longer supplied by the lake, and the water that now usually covers its floor is rainwater. The cave and the fenced-in pump shaft above it are fascinating remnants of the era of the most wonderfully megalomaniacal king Sweden ever had.

# HAGA CASTLE RUIN

## *The remains of a castle that never was*

*The ruin can be accessed via a ladder on the side facing the road below or through an opening in the wall on the other side*
*Metro: Odenplan, then a 30-minute walk*

The basement floor of Haga Castle is all that was built of the grand castle in Haga Park projected by King Gustav III before his death put this project, like so many others, to a grinding halt.

No less than six different architects were commissioned over the years to draw the castle for the king, with inspiration from such diverse European buildings as Marie-Antoinette's Petit Trianon (a small chateau on the grounds of Versailles originally built by Louis XV for his mistress) and Saint Peter's Basilica in Rome.

Climbing down an iron ladder into the ruin today, it has an almost medieval flair and labyrinthine qualities that might make visitors wary a bloodthirsty Minotaur is waiting around the next corner.

The foundation stone was laid in August 1786, probably below the middle pillar. The king, as custom dictated, placed various coins into it, and it was engraved with Latin words stating the king had on this day given freedom back to his people and the castle would be a home for not only freedom, but also pleasure and joy.

The building was planned to contain a sculpture museum, a theatre and ballrooms. Up to 650 soldiers and 150 Russian prisoners of war worked at the building site, though the prisoners were more of a hindrance than a help.

Today a huge and detailed wooden model made a few years after the king's death can be viewed in the nearby little Haga Park Museum (closed in winter).

---

The grimly medieval mood was likely what attracted the black metal band Dark Funeral to use it as the shooting location for the video to their song 'Secrets of the Black Arts' in the winter of 1996. In the video, hooded figures wielding torches do mysterious things in the night.

Due to its secluded location, the ruin was moreover a popular site for clandestine rave parties throughout the 1990s. It has further been used for rituals by many different esoteric groups. The remains of these rituals can sometimes be encountered in the form of burnt-out candles and painted symbols.

Some scenes in the film based on Astrid Lindgren's novel *Ronja the Robber's Daughter* were also shot here in the early 1980s.

# THE MONTELIUS GRAVE

*An odd grave in the style of ancient chieftains*

*Northern Cemetery*
*Lindhagen Hill, quarter 21F, grave 3*
*Cemetery open 24/7*
*Metro: St Eriksplan, then a 20-minute walk*

I n the Northern Cemetery, the resting place of Oscar (1843–1921) and
Agda (1850–1920) Montelius is distinctly archaic-looking. It is designed as a dolmen grave, the type of single-chamber megalithic tomb
common during the Nordic Bronze Age.

Like its ancient archetype, the Montelius tomb has two upright megaliths supporting a large, flat horizontal capstone and is cloaked in grass-covered earth. This is not a random choice, as Oscar was an influential archaeologist who refined the concept of seriation (a relative chronological dating method in archaeology) and also served as National Antiquarian.

In the early 2000s, a journalist claimed Oscar had been a pioneer of scientific racism, specifically via his work on phrenology and craniology, though this has been questioned by historians.

His wife Agda was a philanthropist, feminist and peace activist. The grave certainly looks quite out of place but must be appreciated as the final romantic gesture of a devoted antiquarian, who may or may not have been a racist trailblazer.

There are a great number of fascinating grave markers in the Northern Cemetery, where you can easily spend a whole day strolling. Especially interesting is the hill (Lindhagens kulle) where the Montelius grave stands, as it is home to most of the mausoleums and some of the more spectacular grave markers.

Also worth a look are the cemetery's water basins, designed by architect Peder Clason after an open competition and produced in 1923. The basin sides are decorated with a ship depicted in typical 1920s style, while water flows into them from the mouth of a clumsily sculpted, fish-like creature apparently intended to be a dolphin.

The Northern Cemetery was inaugurated on 9 June 1827 and is the final resting place of many celebrities. Among them are inventor Alfred Nobel (1833–1896) of Nobel Prize fame, and actress Ingrid Bergman (1915–1982), who starred in *Casablanca* (1942). There's also the stark, black wooden cross of author August Strindberg's (1849–1912) grave, with its stern Latin inscription: *O crux ave spes unica* (O hail the cross, our only hope).

# HAGALUNDSPARKEN
# WATER TOWER

(30)

## Where witches gather

*Källvägen 1*
*It is possible to book a visit (via jolandatarot@gmail.com or by calling*
*+46-0739330777) with or without a fortune telling session. The tower is also an*
*interesting sight from outside*
*Metro: Solna Centrum, then a 15-minute walk (or Solna Station, by commuter*
*train, then a five-minute walk)*

Can a bona fide witch practising her magic in a high tower on a hill be real? Well, in Solna it can.

When a railroad was built through the neighbourhood in 1908, the level of the groundwater used for public water supplies sank, forcing the inhabitants to get their water from Lake Mälaren instead. As this was quite inconvenient, a water tower was built.

Designed by the famous architect Ivar Tengbom (who also planned the Högalid Church and the Concert House) in a national romantic style, it originally also held an apartment for the machinist. By the late 1930s, the construction had already become redundant, as water could be supplied from elsewhere. In the 1970s, the existing old houses surrounding it were torn down and high-rises for cheap housing built quickly in their place.

As the protests against this were quite vocal, it was decided to make the buildings blue so they would blend in with the sky. Nicy try, but of course the sky is not really blue that often. Vernacular humour soon dubbed the ugly buildings on the hill 'Blåkulla' (Blue Hill) – which is also the traditional name of the site where witches gather to frolic with Satan, according to Swedish folklore.

## The national witch of Sweden

In 1998, an administrator at Solna municipality received a call from a woman presenting herself as a witch who wanted to rent the tower. At first, he could not stop laughing for several minutes. But this was no prank, and soon a lease had been signed and the witch was installed in the tower. Her name is Rosie Björkman (born 1957), known as the national witch of Sweden, with a popular TV show of her own back in the 90s. Also going by Jolanda the Third, she has authored several books and devised her own Tarot deck. She lives in an ordinary apartment in the same area, describing herself as an environmentalist and spiritual guerrilla fighter presenting alternative systems of governing, promoting an egalitarian society without hierarchy.

Internally, Björkman and her circle of witches have decorated the tower with occult murals in vivid colours (featuring the goddess, owls, dolphins and mystical symbols), altars and various magical instruments and paraphernalia. The ceiling of the octagonal main ritual chamber is around 10 metres high, and the walls are completely uninsulated – meaning the magical activities are confined to the warmer seasons.

# OLLE OLSSON HOUSE MUSEUM

*Old house meets high modernism*

*Spetsgatan 2*
*Wednesdays and Sundays noon–4pm*

The former home of naivist painter Olle Olsson (1904–1972) is a striking example of frilly, 19th-century cottage cuteness juxtaposed with dystopian 1970s modernist brutalism. Both are in fact quite typical of Sweden in their own way, but seldom do they exist so close to one another.

Olsson's villa was built by his grandfather in 1897, and is a beautiful specimen of imaginative wood architecture. The whole area was filled with similar houses at the time, but in a controversial decision the city council decided to tear them down and begin redevelopment in the late 1960s. Olsson was so saddened by the demolition of the quaint neighbourhood, where he had lived his whole life, that he stopped painting. The Olle Olsson house is now a museum dedicated to his artworks and the history of the district. It is worth a visit not only for the naivist art but also for the interesting contrast between building styles.

© Ankara

On the hill above Olsson's house there now stands eight blue 14-storey buildings, each 100 metres long. Erected between 1969 and 1973, they are characteristic examples of the architectural ideas in vogue at the time, which have never been much liked by most Swedes. Many of the tenants of the buildings have been newly arrived immigrants and the area has suffered from a bad reputation due to a high crime rate. In later years, this began to change due to efforts by the city to improve the area by adding more greenery and renovating run-down facilities. That many of the apartments have been converted to private housing cooperatives has also contributed to this positive process (though recent shootings and bomb attacks have once more blackened its reputation).

# FILMSTADEN

*The old film studio lot where Ingmar Bergman worked*

*Greta Garbos väg 3.*
*Friday to Sunday 11am–6pm, guided tours on Sundays*
*Metro: Näckrosen*

Filmstaden ('the cinema city') is the old studio lot from 1920 where many key works in Swedish cinema history were produced. More than 400 films and TV series were shot there before it closed in 1999. Surprisingly, it is little known to Stockholm inhabitants but is open to visitors.

The entrance to Filmstaden, with a wrought-iron portal, still stands. Next to it is the house of the gatekeeper who was responsible for keeping autograph hunters and other fans out, with two big dogs to assist him. He also oversaw the handling of the dangerous nitrate films used during the early days of cinema. Today, this house is a film-themed, retro-style cafe. Walking around the lot, it is easy to imagine the frantic activity of days past, even though all is now rather quiet.

The old laboratory building (now the Swedish offices of Universal Pictures) had a special fire and explosion-safe construction due to the nitrate film. Up to 25,000 metres of film could be processed in a single day and from here, all copies for every cinema in Sweden were distributed.

Inspired by, among other places, Babelsberg film studios in Berlin, the architect Ebbe Crone constructed huge halls with roofs and walls of glass and no supporting pillars in the middle (to facilitate light and space for the film shoots).

In 1919, before the studio lot was even fully finished, the silent classic *The Phantom Carriage* (*Körkarlen*, released 1921) – directed by Victor Sjöström and based on a novel by Selma Lagerlöf – was filmed at Filmstaden. Sjöström was a mentor to Ingmar Bergman, who cut his teeth in the cinema business in this very place. When he later started out as a director, Bergman was, with characteristic modesty, 'convinced that [he] would quickly manifest himself as the world's greatest film director'. More than half of his filmography was shot here.

Among these films was the great classic *Det sjunde inseglet* (*The Seventh Seal*, 1957), finished in only 35 days. The production included several dramatic outdoors scenes, among them the public burning of a witch. Prepared with help from a local fire captain, the scene was witnessed by a huge local audience from the windows and balconies of the high-rise neighbourhood close to Filmstaden.

In commemoration of Bergman's work, a sculpture by Peter Linde has been erected on the lot. Named Teatervagnen (The Theatre Wagon), it features several figures from *Det sjunde inseglet* – among them Death personified and the knight Antonius Block.

# North-East

(1) KAKNÄS PET CEMETERY ................................ 236
(2) THE EYE ON FILMHUSET .............................. 238
(3) ITALIENSKA KULTURINSTITUTET ................ 240
(4) VILLA LUSTHUSPORTEN ............................. 242
(5) SKÅNSKA GRUVAN ................................... 244
(6) BIOLOGICAL MUSEUM ............................... 252
(7) DC-3 79001 HUGIN MEMORIAL STONE ....... 254
(8) WASA GARDEN ......................................... 256
(9) JÄGARHYDDAN ........................................ 258
(10) CAPTIVE VIKING STATUE .......................... 260
(11) SWEDENBORG'S GAZEBO .......................... 262
(12) GIRAFFE CRANE ...................................... 266
(13) SECRETS OF KASTELLHOLMEN ................... 268
(14) THE VIKING SHIP AT THE FORMER SCHOOL OF NAVAL
     WARFARE ............................................... 270
(15) BÅÅTSKA PALATSET ................................. 272
(16) 'DEVIL'S BIBLE' IN THE ROYAL LIBRARY ...... 278
(17) FORMER CZECHOSLOVAKIAN EMBASSY ...... 280
(18) TEKNISKA HÖGSKOLAN METRO STATION ... 282
(19) HIDDEN TREASURES OF THE ROYAL INSTITUTE OF
     TECHNOLOGY ......................................... 288
(20) R1 ...................................................... 292
(21) OWLS OF UGGLEVIKSKÄLLAN ................... 294
(22) FISKARTORPET ...................................... 296
(23) EDELCRANTZ OCTAGONAL TOWER ........... 298

# KAKNÄS PET CEMETERY

*Cats, dogs, a Komodo dragon and a beetle ...*

*Kaknäsvägen 38*
*Open 24/7*
*Bus 69 to Kaknäsvägen. Walk to Kaknäsvägen and continue past Djurgården*
*IP to Lindarängsvägen, then follow the sanded path leading into the forest for*
*around 150 metres*

Tucked away in the forest between the Kaknäs tower and Lidingöbro Inn is Stockholm's pet cemetery, which is more than 100 years old. For long periods, it has not been an officially approved place of burial, but this has not stopped grieving pet owners constantly using it.

The animals buried are mostly cats and dogs, but there are also rats, rabbits, hamsters, tortoises, parrots and even a Komodo dragon. There's even a marked grave for a beetle. Horses have been buried too, includ-

ing the famous police horses Utter and Vanten that were friends in life and now rest next to each other. An even more famous horse having been granted its final resting place there is Don Juan, which the knight Antonius Block (played by Max von Sydow) rode in Ingmar Bergman's legendary film *The Seventh Seal* (*Det sjunde inseglet*, 1957).

The cemetery was created spontaneously after the author August Blanche (1811–1868) buried his dog Nero on the site. Nero had originally been buried in the city, but road construction required a move of the gravestone and urn. This move was heavily reported on by the media in highly sentimental terms, as Blanche was one of the most popular authors of his day. Soon after, others started burying their own dead pets close to Nero's grave.

Today the cemetery is run by retired gardener Erik Westerberg, who read about it in a newspaper more than 30 years ago. At the time, it was not in official use but, after much effort, he managed to get approval for burials and became the cemetery caretaker (in cooperation with the Swedish Kennel Club).

When burying an animal, it first has to be cremated. Upon arrival at the cemetery, the caretaker meets the pet owners. The burial rite starts with him saying a few words about the history of the place, then reading the prayer of St Francis, the patron saint of animals (St Francis, in the

12th and 13th centuries, was famous, among other things, for being able to talk to animals), while the urn with the ashes is placed in the ground. Some people want to have a priest present, or to play some suitable music, both of which can be accommodated.

Many pet owners visit their dear departed companions regularly, and some gravestones are quite lavish. Many must also be said to be rather tacky, but the heartfelt sincerity is often touching. You can easily spend an hour there, reading the inscriptions that range between the absurd and the sad.

# THE EYE ON FILMHUSET

*An ironic Cold War gesture*

*Borgvägen 1*
*Metro: Karlaplan*

**F**ilmhuset is a monumental 1971 brutalist building, with a rather peculiar eye decoration on a difficult-to-see portion of its exterior. Home to, among others, the Swedish Film Institute and Stockholm University's department of Cinema Studies, it was designed by influential architect Peter Celsing.

According to legend, the original design was drawn on a napkin at the Opera Bar when conceptualised by Celsing and the Film Institute director Harry Schein.

Unfortunately, the Swedish military has an office building across from the western short end of Filmhuset and demanded that no windows be allowed on that side. No doubt, their concerns were aggravated by the left-leaning reputation of Swedish film workers and cinema students; they didn't want a bunch of bearded commies directing their binoculars at the military's desks. Celsing complied, but sarcastically commented by add-

ing a gigantic, staring metal eye to decorate the side of the building.

The shining steel eye can only be seen if you stand at the correct angle, not the directions you would normally approach the house from, so it is an amusing little architectural Easter egg unseen by most visitors.

To view it, walk up between Filmhuset and Försvarets materielverk via the semicircular parking space on the western side. If you want to take pictures, be careful that you don't appear to be pointing your camera toward the military facility.

The rest of the building is also filled with playful features, but ones referencing the art of cinema. Window openings on the top floors are reminiscent of the holes perforating a strip of film, as are the half-circle patterns along the sides of the concrete blocks making up the facade of the lower levels. The round stairwells look like rolled-up strips of film when seen from above. The elevator doors are constructed to resemble make-up mirrors. Some of the more impractical decorative details Celsing came up with were eventually removed, for example incredibly thick and rough carpeting in the entrance area that many employees sprained their ankles on, and the pools of slippery marble in the red carpet of the foyer (where the architect envisioned gala premiere guests would dance). A nice new addition is the red zigzag, neon-like lighting added to the ceiling of the long ramp leading up to the entrance, which dissipates some of the oppressive feeling the building can emanate on a grey day.

# ITALIAN CULTURAL INSTITUTE

*A mid-century modernist dream, by Giò Ponti*

*Gärdesgatan 14*
*Open for frequent events, and regular courses. You can view parts of the*
*interior through the big windows of the annex during daytime*
*Metro: Karlaplan*

Designed by Italian master architect Giò Ponti (1891–1979), the Italian (Cultural) Institute is a jewel of mid-century aesthetics both in terms of its striking exterior and the top-quality interior and furnishings.

The institute's location next to the vast, open field Gärdet came about after the Swedish and Italian governments made a bilateral donation of land in Stockholm and Rome, respectively. The intention was to strengthen Swedish–Italian cultural ties by erecting designated buildings for cultural exchange. Stockholm was blessed with this stunning, sleek and discreetly curved building by Ponti (with help from the Swede Ture Wennerholm) and Rome was given the Swedish Institute designed by Ivar Tengbom.

Ponti's creation has been likened both to a ship's hull (in fact, Ponti had worked on designing furniture for transatlantic liners, so the parallel is not far-fetched), and an elegant lady's shoe dropped in the grass. The facade is covered in a white mosaic that glitters enticingly when the sun is out.

Connected to the main building is an annex clad in mustard yellow tiling. It contains a screening and performance space with room for 300 people and has ceiling lighting fixtures cleverly concealed behind a diagonal grid (exactly who designed it is a little unclear: Ponti or his colleague Pier Luigi Nervi).

Ponti also masterminded the choice of furniture, lighting, decorations and materials for the interior. The veteran was not new to working on Italian cultural institutes, having refurbished the 19th-century Fürstenberg Palace in Vienna in 1935. In Stockholm, however, he got to create it from the ground up, and so thoroughly put his stamp on everything that the whole project must be designated a Ponti *Gesamtkunstwerk*. He was devoted not only to architecture but also ceramics, furniture and textile design, painting and other arts. This is something that truly shines through in the Stockholm building he created.

The ground floor of the main building contains offices and a library, the first floor holds lecture theatres and the second floor comprises lodgings for students and the director and vice-director, including a shared kitchen and living area. Pretty much all portions of the interior offer fabulous furniture and textiles; the staircases and their beautifully irregular railings, for example, are works of art.

But the institute is anything but a dry, dead museum. Rather, it is bristling with activity, and it is possible to take courses in Italian or attend frequent exhibitions and events – usually all free.

# VILLA LUSTHUSPORTEN

## One of the most eclectically gorgeous houses in Stockholm

*Rosendalsvägen 3*
*Private, but you can get a good look through the fence at all times of day*
*Metro: Karlapan, then a 15-minute walk*

© Holger Ellgaard

Enclosed behind a high iron fence, the Wicander Villa (also known as Villa Lusthusporten) is one of the most eclectically gorgeous houses in Stockholm, both internally and externally.

Formerly the site of a well-known inn which burned down in 1869, the first version of the present villa was built in Italian style in the 1870s by the merchant Alfred Brinck. The facade was Renaissance-inspired with a side tower. Brinck sold the house to another merchant, Edvard Liljewalch, in 1882. He subsequently passed it to the organisers of the 1897 Stockholm exhibition. In conjunction with the exhibition, the stables, greenhouse and other smaller buildings belonging to the villa were torn down, while the main building functioned as the press pavilion and the cellar was used as a detention centre by the police.

Afterwards, the villa was bought by Hjalmar Wicander (1860–1939), who made a fortune from his cork factories. An art collector with exquisite taste, he had the architect Carl Möller (1857–1933) redesign the villa into a representative home. Möller kept the frame of the old building but transformed it into a creation with traits of Nordic Renaissance architecture, contemporary English villas, and the transnational Jugend/art nouveau style in vogue at the time.

Take a pair of binoculars to be able to appreciate all the whimsical details on the exterior, which is filled with sculpted stone birds, fish and grinning faces.

The interior is also opulent, with oak-panelled walls and a multitude of amusing carved wood figures incorporated into doors and other things. The totality makes for a very Harry Potter-style house, where it would not feel entirely unexpected if one of the carved goblin faces spoke.

When Wicander died in 1939, his will stipulated the house was to be inherited by the Nordic Museum, and it became home to the Institute for Folk Life Research and the department with the same focus from what would become Stockholm University.

At that time, a professor also lived in the house. The villa's special atmosphere was so appealing that some students even chose this discipline primarily because of it. The academics have since left and the house is now rented to a company.

---

The former stable, which has superbly sculpted horse heads above its doors, is today a parent co-op Montessori pre-school.

# SKÅNSKA GRUVAN

*A former mining display, bomb shelter and pavilion
of the 1897 Stockholm exhibition*

*Rosendalsvägen 14*
*Cafe open 9am–3pm most days*
*Metro: Karlapan, then a 15-minute walk*

**S**kånska gruvan (The Scanian Mine) is a capricious and over-the-top
building constructed as one of the pavilions for the 1897 Stockholm exhibition. It has since had a dramatic history. One of several
pavilions for this event designed by architect Gustaf Wickman, today it
is one of only three that remain.

© Frankie Fouganthin

Its style is highly eclectic and combines features from Spanish houses, Renaissance palaces and North American industrial architecture, incorporating some beautiful tiling work in both abstract patterns and with motifs of flowers in vases.

Paid for by the Scaninan region's brick, tile, sugar, chalk, cement and coal industries, you can still discern the company names if you look closely: Cementbolaget on the rail of the staircase, and Höganäs and Maltesholm on the front wall. The building's name is derived from the simulated mine that was its main attraction during the exhibition, attracting some 70,000 visitors.

As part of its display on mining industries, patrons could ride a basket down through the building's tall chimney. The basket moved very slowly, while the walls were covered in cloth that was set in rapid motion

and thus gave the illusion of going deep into a mine shaft. This gimmick was the main attraction.

However, after the Stockholm exhibition was over, the mining display was disassembled in stages, and today nothing of it remains.

Until 1924, the nearby Skansen open-air museum used it for exhibiting part of their collection, but then closed it to the public and used it for storage. During World War II, the spaces extending into the mountain were blasted to expand their volume for use as bomb shelters.

From the 1960s on, the Maritime Museum also stored part of their collections there.

In 1977 the house burnt down, leaving only the walls. The facade was reconstructed to look approximately the same as the original, but with blind windows and no usable structure behind. Only between

© Jopparn

1999 and 2001 was it completely renovated, then reopened to the public. Today it houses a cafe but is very much worth a look even for those not in the mood for coffee.

## A place to secretly store the country's gold reserve?

As urban legend goes, it is said that the Swedish National Bank (Riksbanken) secretly stored the country's gold reserve in Skånska gruvan's depths – something later employees and others have been unable to confirm.

ALLMÄNNA
KONST OCH INDUSTRI-
UTSTÄLLNINGEN
STOCKHOLM
15 MAJ 1897 1 OKT.

## The 1897 Exposition

The General Art and Industrial Exposition of Stockholm of 1897 (*Allmänna konst- och industriutställningen*), also known as The Stockholm Exhibition or The Stockholm World's Fair (*Stockholmsutställningen*), was a world's fair staged in the city.

After a request in 1893 by several Swedish organisations, King Oscar II approved an exposition of art and industry to be held in 1897, the 25th anniversary of his crowning. The 3,722 exhibitors were limited to Sweden, Finland, Norway, Denmark and Russia, although Canada and Germany requested several times to participate.

The exhibition site was on the island of Djurgården, and many of today's structures on the western part of the island are vestiges from the exhibition.

These include Djurgårdsbron, the main bridge to the island, and the Skansens Bergbana (the funicular railway now in the Skansen open-air museum and zoo).

One of the most prominent buildings of the exposition was a spectacular 16,820-square-metre hall in wood, designed by the architect Ferdinand Boberg. Featuring a 100-metre-tall cupola and four minarets, it was demolished after the exposition, like many other pavilions built in non-permanent materials.

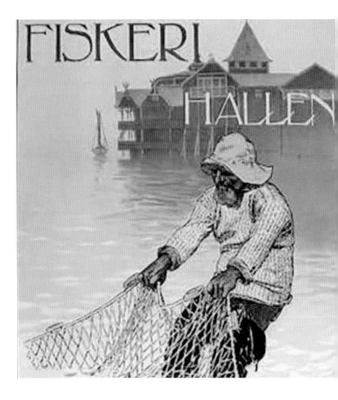

KONST- och INDUSTRI-UTSTÄLLNINGEN i STOCKHOLM 1897.

## What is left of the exposition?

After the closure of the exposition on 3 October 1897, the large industrial hall was torn down with many other pavilions, but some have been preserved.

Still standing in their original places are:

- The Reinhold Bakery, now a restaurant (Wärdshuset Ulla Winbladh).
- The Royal Hunt Club Pavilion, now a private home (see p. 258 – Jägarhyddan).
- The Diamond Rock Drill Co. Pavilion.
- Skånska gruvan (The Scanian Mine) (see p. 244).
- Villa Lusthusporten (see p. 242 – built before 1873, but used as a press pavilion and detention centre during the exhibition).

Several pavilions were moved to Skansen, including the Bragehallen and the Fröstorp.

Others, like the Biologiska museet and the Nordic Museum, were not built specifically for the exhibition but were part of the exhibition area.

Some pavilions were also moved to other locations in Stockholm or nearby, like the Villa Björkudden, which was moved to Tynningsö, in the Stockholm archipelago.

# BIOLOGICAL MUSEUM

*A fascinating, old-style museum with an animal that never existed*

*Hazeliusporten 2*
*biologiskamuseetsvanner.se*
*Open only on special occasions: check website*
*Metro: Karlapan, then a 15-minute walk*

Set to reopen fully in 2025, the biological museum (Biologiska Museet) is a captivating, traditional-style attraction. Its founder, Gustaf Kolthoff (1845–1913), worked as a conservator at the zoology department at Uppsala University and early in life became sceptical about the way museums tended to display stuffed animals in glass cases.

Drawing on Darwin's ideas about adaptation to natural environments, he instead felt they ought to be shown in a context as similar as possible to their actual habitat. For this reason, the 300 or so animals in the museum are quite difficult to spot at times, as one point Kolthoff wanted to make was that they have natural camouflage through their shape and colours. Also, for similar reasons, he opted to have only natural light from the huge overhead windows for most of the displays.

Kolthoff was assisted by his friend and hunting comrade the artist Bruno Liljefors (1860–1939), who painted the backgrounds for the panoramic dioramas the animals are incorporated into. Liljefors was one

© Holger.Ellgaard

of Sweden's most celebrated artists, and their joint efforts made the museum's three floors a curious, dreamlike experience.

Even stranger is the imaginary animal on display on the ground floor: the "skvader", a hare with the back part of a wood grouse. It originates in fanciful hunting tales of a winged hare, told in the 1870s by Håkan Dahlmark in Sundsvall. The creature on display at the museum is of course a whimsical taxidermical assemblage using parts from both animals. Similar fantastical animals are found in Plinius the elder's *Naturalis Historia* (c. CE 77–79), and in US folklore as the "jackalope".

There is also a bear family mounted in a very human-like manner, with the female parent standing and holding one of her cubs by the hand. Neither the skvader nor this are part of Kolthoff's original exhibition.

Kolthoff was backed by several prominent and wealthy patrons, and the plot of land was donated by the king himself. Built in an ornate style inspired by Norwegian stave churches, the museum opened on 11 November 1893 and became an instant success with the public. It was often visited by foreign scientists and sometimes formed part of the programme for state visits.

Kolthoff's radical approach was, however, in question by 1910, when many opined that the museum was outdated and should be moved or torn down (today, this "outdated" dimension is the most fascinating thing about it). This did not happen, but public interest dwindled over the years.

The museum closed to the public in 2017, due to the poor condition of the building and the extremely low number of visitors, but it opens occasionally for special events.

It is set to undergo renovations before a full reopening.

In the meantime, the Friends of the Biological Museum organise a programme on the premises centred around nature, art and climate issues. And the building itself is an amazing sight even from the outside, with its intricately carved wooden front in ancient Norse style.

# DC-3 79001 HUGIN MEMORIAL STONE ⑦

*When Sweden almost went to war with the Soviets in a strange and unresolved shooting*

*Galärvarvet cemetery*
*Djurgårdsvägen 28*
*Open at all times*
*Metro to Karlapan, then a 15-minute walk*

In the Galärvarv cemetery, close to the wall facing The Nordic Museum, a sombre black stone states "In memory and honour of the crew of DC-3 79001 Hugin", followed by a list of names, then "Fallen over the Baltic Sea 13 June, 1952". At the top of the stone, an aircraft is engraved. As Sweden has not been at war for more than 200 years, this may seem peculiar. The DC-3 in question was an unarmed Swedish air force plane shot down in 1952 by Soviet air force fighter jets over international waters in the Baltic Sea, on its way back to Bromma airport.

The incident caused a diplomatic crisis and nearly a full-scale military confrontation. According to Swedish authorities at the time, the Swedes were on a navigation training flight. The plane and its crew vanished without any trace other than a life raft shot full of holes. Three days after the disappearance, two Catalina flying boats were sent to search for it north of Estonia. Again, Soviet aircraft appeared and shot one of them down. Its crew was rescued by a West German freight ship.

Almost 40 years later, it was revealed the DC-3 was in fact carrying British equipment and conducting surveillance for NATO – despite Sweden's "neutral" stance. The Soviet Union long denied responsibility, but in 1991 an official Russian statement sanctioned by President Boris Yeltsin confirmed what had pretty much been known all along: Soviet general Fyodor Shinkarenko ordered MiG-15s to shoot down the DC-3 over international waters.

When divers finally found the wreckage of the plane in 2003, it contained four bodies. What happened to the other four remains an open question. Some theories claim they were picked up by a Soviet torpedo vessel, taken to Tallinn and handed over to Soviet authorities. The widow of one of the crewmen received a postcard from Leningrad in the early 1980s she believed was sent by her husband. There were also unconfirmed claims about four Swedish prisoners in Gulag camps.

It has also been suggested the DC-3's Russian-speaking telegraphist, Erik Carlsson, was a KGB spy who tipped the Soviets off. Security Service documentation confirms Carlsson was suspected of espionage and communist sympathies. The Soviet pilot who fired at the DC-3 said he saw a man leaving the plane in a parachute (though he later retracted this claim). The accusations must therefore be said to rest on very shaky foundations, and Carlsson's name remains with the others on the memorial stone.

# WASA GARDEN

## *A reconstructed 17th-century garden*

*Galärvarvsvägen 14*
*Open all day*
*Metro: Karlapan, then a 15-minute walk*

While hordes of tourists visit the wreck of the Wasa ship, adjacent to the museum building lies a hidden gem: a recreated 17th-century herbal garden.

All plants that grow in it were cultivated in the time when the Wasa ship sunk and include vegetables, medicinal plants and flowers – food and medicine for noblemen, farmers and seamen alike. Among the flower beds are beautifully painted life-size wooden silhouettes of farmers and gardeners of the period. You can stroll through the small garden, touching, smelling and even tasting its bounty. Meandering in the tranquil allotment is truly a banquet for all senses and a great activity for kids.

One of the most important plants you will find is hops, growing along poles standing in rows, the cultivation of which was dictated by Swedish law since the Middle Ages to ensure a steady supply of beer for all social classes. Next to bread, this was the primary fare offered on board a ship like Wasa – a diet that unsurprisingly resulted in scurvy for many sailors on longer trips. You can also see flax, which was used for making clothes and sails and as medicine against cough and stomach pain. Many of the plants in the garden had medicinal uses, and on the ships it was the barber (effectively a type of doctor) who was the custodian of such herbal knowledge.

## 'The head gardener must know that the planets and the 12 signs of the zodiac should correspond in seeding and planting work.'

The garden also has signs with little quotations from historical sources about growing plants, for example, 'In the month of May you must fertilize your cabbage patch and plant enough cabbages so as to last the whole year', from a 1520s almanac. More esoteric is the statement from a Swedish housekeeping handbook from the 1660s: 'The head gardener must know that the planets and the 12 signs of the zodiac should correspond in seeding and planting work.' Another 1660s admonition is also striking: 'The earth is the most important thing we have. Be prepared to feed, fertilize, and treat it well, so that it will have the strength to repay its master for his toils.' These are certainly words that, even today, we would do well to heed.

# JÄGARHYDDAN

*The former Hunter's Hut of the great Stockholm exhibition of 1897*

*Djurgårdsvägen 23*
*Private*
*Metro: Karlaplan, then a 15-minute walk*

Tucked away among the trees on a hillside stands a house that looks like the dwelling place of some mysterious wizard who could step out at any moment pointing his wand to curse you for trespassing. And this is indeed a private villa, that you should not get too close to – but out of politeness, rather than fear of being cursed.

Yet this was not always so, as its wind wane in the shape of a golden huntsman drawing his bow tells us. The figure indicates the original purpose of this singular building: During the great Stockholm exhibition of 1897, it was the shared pavilion of the Royal Hunting Club and the Swedish Hunting League. As such, it was very much open to the public and called *Jägarhyddan* (The Hunter's Hut).

The interior was filled with hunting trophies (including the stuffed head of an elk shot by the king himself), rifles and hunting knives. It also contained a restaurant.

Designed by architect Fredrik Liljekvist, it remained in the possession of the Royal Hunting Club after the exhibition closed but was sold off in 1907. Today it is privately owned.

The interplay of round, square and octagonal shapes densely packed together make this quirky and compact house one of the most eye-catching and imaginative in Stockholm.

Its windows in different shapes and sizes, dark brown wooden panelling contrasting with white plaster coating, and copper roofs in beautifully organic neo-baroque shapes are disparate but somehow merge into a harmonious whole. It is also studded with charming details like the wind wane and the winding stairway with gnarly, untreated tree branches integrated into its railing.

© Holger Ellgaard

# CAPTIVE VIKING STATUE

*A kinky, bondage Viking*

*Opposite Djurgårdsvägen 64*
*Metro: Karlapan, then a 15-minute walk*

Enthusiasm for Sweden's Viking past was rife in the late 19th century. There are traces of this across Stockholm, like the 1903 statue in Mariatorget of a muscular, virile Thor smashing the Middle-earth serpent on the head with his hammer. This Thor is warlike, mirroring the militarisation of the times, and dynamic and vigorous like the businessmen and innovators of the new capitalist society – men of action with no refined, aristocratic manners.

A somewhat different take on Viking masculinity is the statue *Fången Viking* (*Captive Viking*) by John Börjeson (1836–1910). It depicts a naked, slender Viking youth, hands and feet bound, who looks passive and vulnerable but still has an air of defiance about him.

According to the contemporary encyclopaedia *Nordisk familjebok*, Börjeson had 'a special ability to give firmness and resilience to his figures' and 'a developed sense for the masculine'. Yet, not all have conformed to this straight, 'vanilla Viking' understanding of this particular example of his work – for a long time, some people have perceived a homoerotic bondage kink dimension in the statue. A recent example is when it was listed as one of Stockholm's 'truly sexy statues' by gay magazine *Out*.

*Captive Viking* was sculpted by Börjeson in 1878, but not cast until 1913. This means it became one of the last pieces of public art with an ancient Norse theme from this epoch. Interestingly, it came into being far from the frozen north, during Börjeson's years in Paris. It was gifted to the Royal Djurgården Administration by the Jewish businessman Gustav Fränckel, who was the director of the restaurant Hasselbacken, which lies on the hill above the statue. What can in a sense be called the last Viking was thus conceived in France, paid for by a Jewish businessman, and has homoerotic undertones – an amusing subversion of the period's hyper-nationalist framings.

---

In 2016, the statue was included in the art project 'wigs on public art', where the artists chose it because they thought it looked like David Bowie (who had just died). They took pictures of the poor Viking with a wig similar to Bowie's hairdo on the classic album *Alladin Sane* (1973), claiming the sculpture's depiction of the Viking's vulnerable condition correlates with the sense of confinement Bowie experienced at times.

# SWEDENBORG'S GAZEBO

*Where the great mystic talked to angels and demons*

*Skansen open-air museum in Djurgården*
*Close to the recreated 1930s co-op store*
*The gazebo can be viewed from the outside during the normal opening hours of*
*Skansen:*
*May to September, every day 10am–6pm*
*October to April, weekdays 10am–3pm, weekends 10am–4pm*
*Metro: Karlaplan*

According to tradition, Swedenborg's gazebo was where the famous Swedish mystic (see p. 264) had his conversations with angels, demons and spirits of the dead. Swedenborg lived in a small manor house on Hornsgatan 41–43 in Södermalm, which he built for himself around 1750. In 1767 he added a gazebo to his garden. According to a second-hand account of his gardener's wife's statements, Swedenborg beheld his 'visions somehow float towards him' from an ornamented mirror hanging on a wall in the gazebo.

After Swedenborg's death, his nephew – a bishop – bought the house in Södermalm. However, it proved difficult to rent it out as he had planned, since people thought it was haunted. The main building thus fell into disrepair and was torn down. The gazebo was used for storage and subsequently became a hideout for thieves. For a period, a poor widow and her many children lived there.

Pandering to the period's taste for the Gothic and morbid, it then opened to the public as a ghoulish display room. The walls were covered in black cloth strewn with silver stars, and the centrepiece was a coffin with a wax doll of Swedenborg. This tasteless spectacle could be viewed for the sum of 10 öre, much to the disgust of several prominent foreign visitors (including US president Ulysses Grant in 1878), who found it difficult to understand why the last remaining building from the home of the internationally famous mystic was not being preserved in a more dignified manner.

When Hornsgatan was going to be broadened towards the end of the 19th century, the gazebo had to be removed. Swedenborgians in Sweden and abroad failed in an effort to raise money to build a church on the site. In 1896, the creator of the open-air museum Skansen stepped in, buying the gazebo for 500 Swedish crowns. It was originally placed close to the tower Bredablick in Skansen and moved to its present location in the 1960s.

## Two other replicas of the gazebo

There are two replicas of the gazebo in the inner city. One was built in 1989 and placed close to where Swedenborg's house once stood. It is used by the tenants of the present-day apartment block, but is also rented for events by different Swedenborg organisations. It is not open to the public.

A second replica is placed next to the Swedenborgian church in Vasastan (see p. 156).

## Emanuel Swedenborg (1688–1772), Sweden's foremost mystic

Emanuel Swedenborg is probably Sweden's most famous esotericist and mystic of all time. He first established himself as a respected scientist and inventor. Among other things, he was a member of two of the country's scientific societies with royal patronage: the Royal Academy of Sciences and the Royal Society of Sciences in Uppsala. As an inventor, he tried to design a submarine, a machine gun and a flying machine.

A pivotal moment in Swedenborg's spiritual development occurred in April 1745 while he was dining at a London inn. This is how he recounted the event: "Towards the end of the meal I noticed a sort of dimness in my eyes, it was getting dark, and I saw the floor covered with the most hideous crawling animals, such as snakes, frogs and similar creatures …". He then saw a man sitting in a corner who gave the following exhortation to Swedenborg: "Don't eat so much!" This statement certainly seems somewhat prosaic, considering what followed. The same night the person reappeared, now in Swedenborg's dreams. He declared that he was God himself, that he had chosen the Swedish scientist to reveal the true, hidden messages of the Bible and that he would guide Swedenborg in what to write. This resulted in the eight-volume work *Arcana Cælestia* (*Heavenly Secrets*, 1749–1756), followed by a series of further books.

His experiences culminated in a "spiritual awakening" in which he received a revelation that Jesus Christ had appointed him to write The Heavenly Doctrine to reform Christianity. According to The Heavenly Doctrine, the Lord had opened Swedenborg's spiritual eyes so that from then on he could freely visit heaven and hell to converse with angels, demons and other spirits.

There are several well-known stories about Swedenborg's psychic abilities. One is about how, by communicating with the spirit of a dead person, he miraculously recovered some lost papers. Another reports how he was able to tell Queen Lovisa Ulrika the last words spoken to her by her dead brother that no one else knew. A third describes how Swedenborg sat at a dinner party in Gothenburg and became extremely worried about a fire he claimed had just broken out near his home on Södermalm in Stockholm. After a while, he calmed down and announced that the fire had been stopped three blocks from his house. The other guests were not convinced by what he said, but two days later a dispatch arrived from Stockholm confirming that everything had happened exactly as he described. He is also said to have predicted the day of his own death.

Swedenborg's massive works are often grandly cosmic. He describes in detail the nature of various hells and heavens, journeys into space and visits to other planets, conversations with aliens, angels and demons. But his visionary project also had concrete earthly implications. For example, in some places in his writings he seems to be an early advocate of vegetarianism (although elsewhere he could write about meat-eating as unproblematic). He was probably more or less a vegetarian himself. This led many of his later followers to make the same choice.

One issue he was very concerned about was the ideal marriage, where the man should be an earthly manifestation of wisdom, while the woman manifested love. If this duality was handled correctly, the marriage became strong – potentially so strong that it continued even after physical death.

Swedenborg's books were published in Amsterdam and London, as Sweden had strict censorship of unconventional religious texts. He gained followers at home and abroad, but only in 1874, after changes in legislation, could a Swedish Swedenborg Church (see p. 156) operate fully in the open.

In 1818, a priest in the Swedish State Church expressed Swedenborgian sympathies and was defrocked, as the ideas constituted heresy. Many Swedish authors were nonetheless influenced, including greats like Per Daniel Amadeus Atterbom (1790–1855), Carl Jonas Love Almqvist (1793–1866) and August Strindberg (1849–1912). Foreign celebrities like Honoré de Balzac (1799–1850), Victor Hugo (1802–1885), and William Blake (1757–1827) also embraced his ideas.

Swedenborg's bicentennial in 1888 was celebrated with church services, a commemorative plaque on Hornsgatan and a gala dinner at the Grand Hôtel. In 1885, a street in Södermalm was named after him in connection with the major street name revision in Stockholm.

In 1908, he was buried in Uppsala Cathedral, indicating that the Church of Sweden had by then become somewhat reconciled to his ideas.

# GIRAFFE CRANE

*A whimsical crane like no other*

*Beckholmen*
*The best view is from the top of the little mountain on Beckholmen, or from the pier on the Djurgården side*
*Metro: Karlapan, then a 20-minute walk*

© Matti Blume

Standing by the shoreline on Beckholmen is a true oddity: a 100-tonne crane painted with a giraffe pattern.

Originally built when Stockholm was very much a port city, it is a landmark from the period when the city's economic growth was entirely dependent on import and export via the sea. But it is also a symbol of the whimsy of Swedish artists.

Initially one of two cranes placed close to Skeppsbron and Stadsgården, in the late 1980s they belonged to the steel wholesalers the Edstrand brothers and stood in Södra Hammarbyhamnen.

One day, the artist Tor Svae (born 1945) walked past and thought they looked very much like a pair of giraffes. He decided he would indeed turn them into such with an ambitious paint job and got in touch with the owners – who agreed. Not long after, however, the Edstrand brothers closed down operations in Hammarbyhamnen, and the city needed the spaces where the cranes stood. They were therefore to be cut down and the remains sent to the junkyard. Svae, who describes himself as "the banner-carrier of childlikeness" (and has also designed playgrounds and furniture for children), got in touch with a local politician and managed to get the funding intended for the cost of scrapping the cranes to use for moving them instead.

Named Tor and Freja (after the ancient Norse gods) by Svae, the cranes gained a group of admirers who helped form the Friends of the Giraffes in 1992. Sadly, Freja became so worn out that it had to be scrapped in the end. Until quite recently, Tor remained in action at a repair wharf. But time caught up even with the mighty Tor, which was deemed too weak and too limited in reach. Luckily, it could be retired from active work and moved to a different location, living on as an art installation and a memorial over the port epoch. Some plates on the neck of the giraffe had by then been blown off by the wind, but it remained structurally sound.

The present plan is to turn the 'belly' of the crane into a small conference and eating space. Through renting it out for such occasions, the Friends of the Giraffes intend to secure the necessary funding to keep it in shape. Svae also plans to make miniature giraffe cranes to sell as souvenirs to tourists – which is certainly more fun than the mandatory Dala horse!

# SECRETS OF KASTELLHOLMEN ⑬

*A whimsical royal monogram and single-person bunkers*

*Örlogsvägen 5*
*Metro: Kungsträdgården, then a 15-minute walk*

C lose to the bridge connecting Kastellholmen and Skeppsholmen is the Royal Ice Skating Pavilion. Look for the royal monograms on its wall, where Queen Sofia's (1836–1913) has a surprising pair of ice skates hanging from it!

Built in 1882 for upper-echelon people to skate on the frozen lake below and keep warm and drink hot chocolate, this was the place to be during winter for members of high society. Today it is a conference centre and can be rented for events. It is possible to have a look at the impressive interior through its large windows.

Kastellholmen (the castle islet) derives its name from the small, castle-like building that in 1845 replaced an older, similar structure after its destruction due to an accidental explosion in the gunpowder storage below it. Since 1665, the Swedish naval ensign is raised there every

morning to show that Sweden is not at war and Stockholm is not occupied by foreign forces. The castle is especially atmospheric at night when lit by spotlights from below.

Another reminder of the islet's military past is the single-person cast-iron bunkers scattered around it. Looking like oversized black knight's helmets with a little door, these claustrophobic constructions would have protected against bullets and possibly grenades, but hardly against artillery.

## A cross from the secretive order Arla Coldinu

On one of the islet's high points, a big metal cross is mounted on a pole. This is one of several such crosses placed on various sites in the archipelago by the secretive order Arla Coldinu. With strong ties to Swedish high nobility, it claims to have its origins in a medieval naval order from the Mediterranean area, but reveals the exact origin and the meaning of its name only to members that hold the highest degrees.

For more on the order, see the separate entry on p. 123.

## Submerged shipwrecks

Surrounding the islet are around 30 shipwrecks. Usually they are not visible from land, but at times the water level becomes so low that at least one of them, about 10 metres from the western shore, can be seen (on rare occasions, even protruding from the water). This ship is probably the *Graa Ulv* (The Grey Wolf), a 1640s Danish military vessel conquered by the Swedes.

# THE VIKING SHIP AT THE FORMER ⑭ SCHOOL OF NAVAL WARFARE

*A surreal manifestation of turn-of-the-century nationalism*

Holmamiralens väg 10
Metro: Kungsträdgården, Gamla stan or T-Centralen

The former School of Naval Warfare (Sjökrigsskolan) is an impressive building with a surreal feature: on its side facing the sea, a big Viking ship emerges from its facade.

The Royal Swedish Naval Academy was a school for training officers in the Swedish navy, which operated in various forms between 1756 and 1987. Skeppsholmen had been a home to Swedish navy facilities since 1640. In 1756 a permanent wharf was built here, and the place remained the navy's base of operations in Stockholm until the 1960s.

From 1867, the Naval Academy functioned as a basic training school for officers, with cadets typically aged 13 to 16 when they began their six-year education. For this purpose, a building (designed by Axel Fredrik Nyström) was built between 1878 and 1879. It contained lecture halls, a mess and a skylight observatory.

As it was built in the midst of Swedish nationalistic fervour, the many exterior decorations reflect the overblown national pride of the period. The names of various Swedish naval heroes are inscribed on the facade, which also bears the Lesser Coat of Arms of Sweden and the royal monogram of King Oscar II.

More bizarre is the stern of a Viking ship, featuring a winged dragon figurehead thrown in for good measure. Vikings were at the time lauded as bold seafarers and brave warriors in patriotic poetry and art, and functioned as romantic role models for those wishing to instil national pride in their countrymen. Today, it makes a peculiar impression, as if time-travelling Vikings have crashed through the building with their flying ship and become petrified by some sinister magician.

In 1943, the Royal Swedish Naval Academy moved to Täby, and the building on Skeppsholmen became an administrative navy centre. It houses a private research centre.

By 2013, many of the figures and ornaments had been severely damaged by frost and age, and the building underwent extensive renovations. Much of it had to be recreated using entirely new moulds, in a complex process that must be deemed a great antiquarian success.

# BÅÅTSKA PALATSET

*Main lodge of the Swedish Order of Freemasons*

*Blasieholmsgatan 6*
*Private guided tours can be arranged via the order's website: frimurarorden.se/kontakt*
*The courtyard is open during daytime and quite late most nights*
*Metro: Kungsträdgården*

**B**uilt between 1662 and 1669 for the Lord High Treasurer of Sweden, Seved Bååth, the Bååtska palatset (The Bååth Palace) has been owned by the Freemasons since 1874. Now the Main Lodge of The Swedish Order of Freemasons, it can be visited during private guided tours. One of the standout spaces is the Knight's Hall, decorated in neo-Gothic style with tall arched pillars (in fact made from concrete rather than stone) and with walls covered by the coats of arms of high-ranking Freemasons.

Also impressive is the Throne Room, with the throne where King Oscar II sat when he inaugurated the palace in the 1870s and a grand stucco ceiling featuring a more recent painting as its centrepiece. Below ground is the Masonic archive, which contains many rare books, documents and manuscripts, including hand-illuminated alchemical works.

The archive is open for scholars to visit after making an appointment with the librarian.

## Freemasonry in Sweden

Freemasonry has its roots in guild-like groups of medieval cathedral builders that guarded the craft secrets of masonry from outsiders by employing passwords and special handshakes. Over time, it developed into a fraternal system for self-development focused on theatrical initiation rituals and started welcoming non-craftsmen. It was established in Sweden in 1735. Elsewhere, it has often been anti-clerical and republican, whereas Swedish Freemasonry has, by contrast, maintained an excellent relationship with the Church of Sweden (counting several bishops among its brothers) and always having a member of the royal family as its grandmaster from the mid-18th century until 1997.

In more recent years, the order has been trying to get away from its reputation as a secretive and suspicious organisation, even making its membership records and member magazine public. The rituals themselves remain secret, as the pedagogical function of surprise effects for initiates would otherwise be ruined (though one minute on Google would of course reveal them to the curious).

## A Freemason flag

From afar, you can see the white flag with the red Masonic cross flying above the baroque palace, though most will not be aware that it is a Masonic symbol.

© Mats Gärdfors

© Mats Gärdfors

# 'DEVIL'S BIBLE' IN THE ROYAL LIBRARY

## *A legendary tome with a diabolical portrait*

*Royal Library*
*Humlegårdsgatan 26*
*Monday to Thursday 9am–7pm, Friday 9am–6pm, Saturday 11am–3pm*
*Metro: Östermalmstorg*

In a specially designated room deep below the Royal Library lies a huge handwritten Bible containing a full-page portrait of the Devil himself. As you enter the library, walk straight ahead and descend the stairway in front of you two floors.

Supposedly the world's biggest preserved handwritten book, the *Codex Gigas* is written on 310 sheets of parchment, measures 89 by 49 cm and weighs 75 kg. The wooden cover, which is likely original, was clad in white leather by a Stockholm bookbinder in 1819 and has corner clasps decorated with facing gryphons.

Unfortunately, for conservation reasons, we cannot flip through the book and it is always shown closed.

Written in Bohemia (today the western part of the Czech Republic) between 1204 and 1230, it is unknown exactly where and by whom.

The *Codex* eventually ended up in the collection of the esoterically inclined Emperor Rudolph II in Prague (see from the same publisher the book *Secret Prague*), who "borrowed" it from a monastery. When the Swedish army sacked Prague during the Thirty Years' War (1618–1648), it was taken to Stockholm together with a score of other valuables. In 1697, the Royal Castle burnt down, but the book was saved by someone throwing it out of a window, supposedly hitting a person below (who was badly hurt). It was subsequently returned to the Royal Library when a new castle was built.

According to an 1858 book, the caretaker of the library was accidentally locked in after falling asleep and witnessed a startling scene where books floated around in the air, with the "Devil's Bible" knocking down smaller volumes. The experience resulted in the poor man's incarceration in a madhouse.

The *Codex Gigas* was dragged on a sleigh to the recently finished new Royal Library in Humlegården on New Year's Day in 1878, as the final item from the castle library – a symbolic act orchestrated by the head librarian and occultist Gustaf Klemming (a bust of whom can be seen in the entrance to the library).

## *The legend of the* Codex Gigas

Already in the Middle Ages, a legend arose that the book had been produced by a monk who had been walled in due to his sins and tried to redeem himself by creating the world's largest Bible in a single night. As the task understandably proved overwhelming, he called on the Devil for help. In return, the Devil got his portrait painted in the book and later claimed the monk's soul. Luckily, the Virgin Mary intervened at the last minute, just before the monk died.

# FORMER CZECHOSLOVAKIAN EMBASSY

## *Communist brutalist bizarreness*

*Floragatan 13*
*The building is not open to the public, but you can peek in through the big*
*windows to admire the interior*
*Metro: Stadion*

A spectacular example of brutalist architecture, the former Czech-oslovakian Embassy stands as a bizarre alien (well, Central European modernist) artefact among the quaint 19th-century and timid functionalist buildings making up most of its surroundings. It is incredibly well-made, with handcrafted, sculptural concrete walls and first-class materials.

Designed by Jan Bočan, who was only 30 at the time, it was completed in 1970 and is a brutalism fan's wet dream – all concrete and hard angles.

The employees of the embassy during the time of strict communism were not allowed to move around freely in Stockholm. Therefore, the building was equipped with a cinema, a laundry room, garage and gym, to keep everyone within its four walls at (almost) all times.

Even the architect himself was subject to these restrictions, and during meetings with the local builders a party representative always accompanied him. The pressure put on the young man was in fact so high that he suffered a heart attack. Despite this, he would later mention the house as his personal favourite from a long and distinguished career. Together with his colleague Jan Sramek, he designed the furniture and fittings as well, with tables and chairs produced by the legendary Thonet. Some of the seating was quite uncomfortable, and the architect would in his old age admit he knew nothing of ergonomics but simply thought they looked good.

After Czechoslovakia's partition into the Czech Republic and the Slovak Republic in 1992, the Czechs retained the house until 1998. The initial plan was then to tear out the interior and create a more contemporary private office building. Luckily, the communication business that bought it, Kreab, employed the architects Magnus and Olga Tengblad who were intimately acquainted with Bočan – Olga having worked in his office in Prague and Magnus having been visiting professor at the university where he later taught.

This meant the renovation was done with great respect for the original vision. However, some of the unpleasant features necessitated by cold war paranoia – such as the ambassador's office having no windows, to keep snooping capitalists/imperialists from spying on him – were remedied and the total window surface became four times as large.

Today, the building is home to fashion brand Acne. It retains plenty of original furnishings and sci-fi-style lighting fixtures in the ceilings.

# TEKNISKA HÖGSKOLAN METRO STATION

*Cosmic 1970s art*

5am–1am
*Metro: Tekniska högskolan*

Inaugurated in 1973, Lennart Mörk's (1932–2007) decorations at Tekniska högskolan metro station are among the most visionary and evocative in the entire subway system. The station is firmly rooted in the time period it was created, and is reminiscent of certain record covers from that age, for example those of experimental German electronic outfit Tangerine Dream. One can almost hear thick swathes of Moog synthesizer melodies pouring forth when taking the escalators down. Mörk's background as a scenographer (he worked, for example, with Ingmar Bergman) is quite obvious, as this is a total environment in a way that few other metro stations are.

Since it is named after and lies beneath the Royal Institute of Technology (established in 1827, at the present site since 1917), Mörk intended the decor to describe the elements, the laws of nature and how man has always struggled to create order from chaos. The immediate source of inspiration is Plato's concept of the four elements, plus ether as a fifth basic building stone of the universe.

Each is represented by a polyhedron, a body whose sides and angles are all the exact same size. Anyone who has played Dungeons and Dragons in their youth will also recognise them as the exotic-looking types of dice used in role-playing games (eight-sided, four-sided, and so on).

Air is represented by an eight-sided polyhedron made of metal, painted in blue and white. On its sides, there is an aeroplane, the fossil of a prehistoric bird, and a newly hatched seagull. Fire is represented by a four-sided polyhedron, made from concrete sprayed on nets and beams. Painted in vivid red, it depicts the sun giving energy as well as burning, thus creating a continuous cycle. Earth is represented by a six-sided cube, made from net and concrete and painted in browns. Potatoes and sprouts can be discerned, along with an archipelago landscape. Water is represented by a 20-sided polyhedron made from metal. In the ocean painted on it, an oil rig can be seen. At the time it was created, Norwegian off-coast drilling for oil was causing considerable controversy in Sweden. Ether, finally, is represented by a 12-sided polyhedron made from glass, hung from the middle of the ceiling in the middle of the platform. Inside it is a representation of a collapsing star turning into a black hole. It should be looked at from straight below, as the black hole is constituted by a tube. The big spiral inside the glass structure shows how planets are affected by the proximity of the black hole. Shortly after the station opened, one of the glass sheets crashed to the ground below. While this was likely caused by the vibrations coming from the passing trains, it fittingly illustrated the destructive and displacing force of a black hole.

The subway station also contains tributes to great men of science, like Swede Christopher Polhem (1661–1751), an inventor known as the "Archimedes of the North". At one end, Nicolaus Copernicus' (1473–1543) plan of our solar system is shown. Other non-Swedes being celebrated include Leonardo da Vinci (1452–1519) and Isaac Newton (1642–1727). The latter is evoked via a gigantic plaster apple hanging down from the ceiling. This, of course, refers to how Newton came up with his theory of gravity by being witness to an apple falling from a tree. A wing hanging elsewhere in the ceiling represents the wing of Daedalus – perhaps a warning to the physicists, chemists and engineers above against hubris. Nature can and will stop men who attempt to break too drastically with its laws.

Even though these are spectacular decorations, Lennart Mörk had something even more wild in mind at first: His original plan had depictions of the four elements using real fire, real water, electrical aurora borealis and real soil with plants growing in it. This was deemed too costly to maintain, and he had to settle for a compromise. But what a compromise it is! Put some krautrock or 70s electronica in your earphones and walk around Tekniska högskolan subway station for a truly immersive, psychedelic experience.

## Winner of the Kasper Salin Prize

In 1973, Lennart Mörk's work on the station earned him the prestigious Kasper Salin Prize, which is awarded by the Society for Swedish Architects to the year's best buildings.

For more information about Plato's five solids, see the following double page.

# The five basic solides and sacred geometry

Sacred geometry is a world vision according to which the basic criteria for existence are perceived as being *sacred*. Through them can be contemplated the *Magnum Misterium*, the Universal *Grand Project*, by learning its laws, principles and the inter-relationships of shapes. These universal shapes are systematised in a geometric complex in which each figure has its own mathematical and philosophical interpretation. They are applied in projects of *sacred architecture* and *sacred art*, which always use the "divine" proportions in which Man reflects the Universe, and vice versa. It is a common belief that *sacred geometry* and its mathematical relationships, which are harmonic and proportional, are also found in Music, Light and Cosmology. Man first discovered this system of values in prehistoric times, in the megalithic and Neolithic cultures, for example, and some consider it to be a universal facet of the human condition.

*Sacred geometry* is fundamental to the construction of sacred structures, such as synagogues, churches and mosques, and also plays a role in creating the interior sacred space of temples, through the altars and tabernacles. Passed down from Graeco-Egyptian culture and exported to ancient Rome, *sacred geometry* in the European Middle Ages inspired the creation of the Roman and Gothic architecture of Europe's medieval cathedrals, which incorporate this geometry of sacred symbolism.

It is said that Pythagoras (Samos, c. 570 BCE – Metapontum, c. 497 BCE) was the one who founded the system of *sacred geometry* in his school in Croton, Greece. This Greek philosopher and mathematician is believed to have brought the knowledge he acquired in Egypt and India back to Greece.

Using the golden ratio (1.618) and applying it to the geometric forms of the five basic solids, Pythagoras created the mathematical method universally known as *Pythagorean geometry*.

To create the five solids (the tetrahedron or pyramid, the hexahedron or cube, the octahedron, the dodecahedron and the icosahedron), about which Plato would later philosophise (to such a point that they would become known as the *five Platonic solids*), Pythagoras was inspired by the Greek myth about the child-god Dionysus' toys: a basket, dice, top, ball and mirror. On a cosmic level, the *basket* represents the Universe; the *dice*, the *five Platonic solids* symbolising the natural elements (ether, air, fire, water, earth); the *top* is the atom of matter; the *ball*, the Earth's globe; and, finally, the *mirror* reflects the work of the Supreme Geometrist (*Dionysus*), which itself is the universal manifestation of Life and Consciousness, of God towards Man and vice versa.

Each of the five Platonic solids also represents a planetary energy that is connected by its form to a natural element. Thus, the *dodecahedron* is traditionally linked to Venus and ether, the natural quintessence, expressed by a temple's dome. The *octahedron*, linked to Saturn and the air, represents the transept's cross. The tetrahedron, linked to Mars and fire, is symbolised by the openings in the temple through which light gushes forth. The *icosahedron*, linked to the moon and water, establishes the harmony of forms in the temple *design*, constructing the connecting lines between the altars and columns. Finally, the *hexahedron* (cube), fixes the Sun to its element, the Earth, by determining the shape of the temple's foundation or floor.

The main purpose of *sacred geometry* is thus to create Universal Perfection through perfect mathematical forms and calculations, and, by using *sacred architecture*, to connect the Multiple to the Single in a space that is geometrically dedicated to this end.

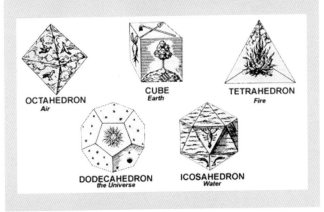

OCTAHEDRON
Air

CUBE
Earth

TETRAHEDRON
Fire

DODECAHEDRON
the Universe

ICOSAHEDRON
Water

# HIDDEN TREASURES
# OF THE ROYAL INSTITUTE
# OF TECHNOLOGY

*A campus full of quirky and pretty decorations*

*Brinellvägen 8*
*The buildings are open during normal office hours – the exterior can be viewed at any time of day*
*Metro: Tekniska högskolan*

Founded in 1827, the Royal Institute of Technology (Kungliga Tekniska Högskolan, KTH) is among Europe's leading technical and engineering universities. Its 1917 campus is full of quirky and pretty decorations that are great fun to discover.

Flanking the main entrance are two chunky stone sculptures of Cerberus-style three-headed dogs. They were created by Carl Milles, a famous artist and devoted spiritualist who claimed to have undergone several paranormal experiences. The unusual choice to have two, rather than one of these hellish hounds, also includes the detail that one of them is female. On the arch above the entrance, Milles depicts man's struggle with the four elements: earth, fire, air, and water.

Another allegorical work is Axel Törneman's 1918 fresco ceiling painting *De elektriska strömmarna* (*The Electrical Currents*), where male and female figures floating on clouds are grouped together in gender-segregated clusters that look much like some sort of homosexual orgy. A colloquial name for the room it can be found in is therefore "porrsalen" (the porn hall). A remarkable aspect of its history is that after KTH was renovated in the 1950s, it was believed for around 40 years that the 217-square-metre painting had been eradicated. Then, in 1993, it was rediscovered, hidden but intact under the new inner ceiling. It was decided to transfer it to a different hall, E1 (also known as Törnemansalen). The process of removing the 0.5-mm layers of paint and gluing them in place in a new location ended up costing five times the sum Törneman was paid back in the day.

## Barack Obama's bathroom

A more recently created peculiar sight is the plaque commemorating US president Barack Obama's visit to KTH – more specifically, his visit to one of the bathrooms on whose door the plaque is mounted. The texts proudly states "U.S. President Barack Obama sat here Sept 4, 2013". University officials did not come up with this idea, and it is likely to be the work of humorous students. Some, however, claim the president used to carry such signs around with him and install them as a joke, an explanation that seems somewhat less likely even if Obama is known to be an amusing man.

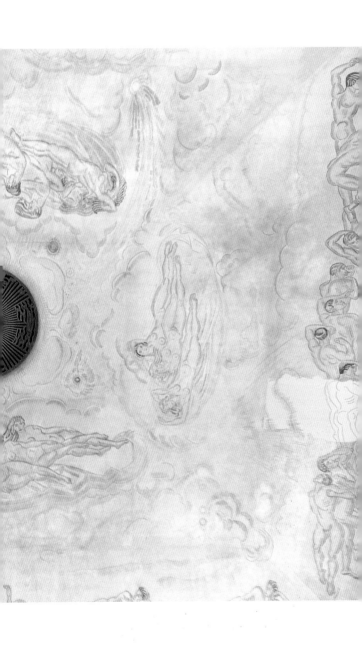

# R1

## *A former experimental nuclear reactor*

*Drottning Kristinas väg 51*
*Check website for dates: kth.se/om/mot/r1/kth-s-reaktorhall-1.739170*
*Open for frequent art and music events. Can also be rented*
*Metro: Tekniska högskolan*

Visiting the disused nuclear reactor R1 underneath Östermalm is like visiting a futuristic off-world mining colony. Accordingly, when entering the anonymous doorway and going 25 metres down into the mountain on the massive beaten-up industrial elevator, it is easy to think of the scene in James Cameron's *Aliens* (1986) where Bill Paxton exclaims: "We're on an express elevator to hell, going down!"

The reactor itself is no longer in place, but the control room (including the board used to control the reactor) is back in place (having returned after a stint at the Technical Museum).

In the middle of the floor is a big hole where the reactor used to be.

But why put a reactor in the middle of a residential neighbourhood to begin with? The explanation lies in how urgent the project was deemed, and expedience dictated it be built in proximity to the Royal Institute of Technology (KTH). The reactor was only used for research purposes and to produce medical isotopes.

After borrowing three tonnes of uranium from France, the reactor was started for the first time on 13 July 1954, at exactly 18.59 hours, and closed on Sweden's National Day (6 June) in 1970. It was then left vacant for many years, though drunken KTH students were rumoured to occasionally make it down there for wild after-parties.

Today the empty reactor hall – still packed with railings, pipes and cranes – is used for art events, as a science lab, and serves as a museum covering Sweden's early nuclear history.

Described by scientists of the time as a "cathedral of science and technology", it now fittingly has its own organ permanently in place – a 1926 Wurlitzer, formerly installed in the Skandia Cinema on Drottninggatan. Indeed, the tall concrete space does resemble a cathedral and has very interesting acoustics. The ceiling was painted blue to give those who worked there a feeling of open sky above them and keep claustrophobia in check. The spray-painted grid you see everywhere inside was used after decommissioning to measure radiation and confirm the whole site was below release limits.

R1 has appeared in movies and music videos like Alan Walker's 2016 "Faded (Restrung)" and Madonna's 1998 hit "Nothing Really Matters".

# OWLS OF UGGLEVIKSKÄLLAN

*A turn-of-the-century pavilion for a sacred spring*

*Uggleviksvägen*
*Ugglevikskällan is open all day*
*Metro: Tekniska högskolan, then a 20-minute walk*

**A** picturesque wooden structure erected in 1902, the Ugglevikskällan pavillion is an octagonal yellow wooden structure decorated with quirky owls – in reference to the name of the spring it was built around, which means "Owl Bay Spring" (derived from the nearby *Uggleviken*, "Owl Bay", which is home to a sizeable population of different kinds of owls).

Documented in textual sources only since the late 18th century, it has been claimed that the spring was considered a sacred place in pre-

historic times and was the object of ancient cultic practices involving sacrifices.

As one of several so-called *trefaldighetskällor* (trinity springs) in Sweden, folklore considered it to have healing powers. These were said to be especially potent if its water was drunk on the night before Trinity Sunday (seven days after Pentecost), preferably in a dose of seven gulps. A ritualistic washing of an ill person was also an option. The water in such a spring should run toward the north, which was seen as the dwelling place of evil and to which the illness could therefore be returned with the flowing water.

Drinking or washing the body were not exclusive to people with health issues, but were primarily a yearly preventative rite. These notions are medieval in origin and coloured by Catholicism, but may also have pre-Christian, pagan roots. It was common to make small sacrificial gifts at the springs well into the 20th century, typically of metal objects like coins or needles.

In the late 19th century, big crowds gathered at Ugglevikskällan on the night before Trinity Sunday to drink its water, dance and have fun. People also came on other occasions, and the water was considered health-bringing even by more rational people who did not believe in the folklore surrounding it.

The pavilion has a shingled roof and benches on both sides. The latter were intended for people to sit on while drinking the miraculous water from the wellspring. However, in the 1970s the water quality deteriorated and it is to-day undrinkable.

The place nevertheless retains its magical atmosphere, and water still breaks forth a bit further on from the old spring – in quantities at least making it possible to go there on the night before Trinity Sunday and wash your hands (but don't drink it!). Better to keep at least this part of your body healthy than to do nothing, right?

# FISKARTORPET

*A king's fishing cabin merged with an ancient tree*

*Norra Fiskartorpsvägen 100*
*Private, but you can look in through the windows*
*Metro: Universitetet, then a 15-minute walk*

Built as a fishing cabin for King Charles XI (1655–1697), Fiskartorpet is a picturesque little house that has slowly merged with the oak tree next to it. As it is forbidden to cut down oak trees in Djurgården (today a national park), the tree is over 330 years old and started growing around the time the house was built. Its roots stretch in under the structure itself and, over the years, the tree has slowly shifted the building. The trunk and branches have also partially grown into the outer walls and the eave, resulting in a fascinating house/tree hybrid.

Its exterior, with a charming turf roof, has hardly changed since it was built. One of the rooms is furnished with rough, old wooden chairs and a table, while the other is more or less empty.

The cabin was documented quite early, being marked on a 1696 map of the area. At the time it was the only building there and the water levels were higher than today, placing this isolated cabin right next to fine fishing waters, where the stressed-out monarch could indulge in some relaxing angling.

It was King Charles XI that created the huge hunting park Djurgården, where the cabin is located, in the 1680s. At first it was wholly a forest and agricultural landscape, but it was transformed to accommodate hunting the almost 1,500 deer placed there. The hunting was partly intended to hone the martial skills necessary in the troubled times Charles XI ruled, when Russia was a constant threat to Sweden.

During the 18th century, a royal gamekeeper lived in the fishing cabin during the summer. There was also an inn on the premises that was popular with the famous composer and poet Carl Michael Bellman (1740–1795). In fact, Bellman was so fond of the place and its beautiful natural surroundings that he mentions it in his song "Fredman's Epistel no. 71", calling it "Divine to behold!"

The fishing cabin and its immediate surroundings have been described as the birthplace of Sweden's infatuation with outdoors culture. The notion of nature as a source of recreation slowly spread to the populace. In the 19th century, the idyllic area around the fishing cabin was chosen as a primary site for the activities of organisations focused on promoting outdoor life – perhaps because the king, with his low-key fishing hangout, was perceived as a pioneer of such things.

# EDELCRANTZ OCTAGONAL TOWER

*An 18th-century optical telegraph station and orangery*

Stora skuggans väg 9
Closed to the public, but you can look in through the windows
Metro: Universitetet, then a 15 minute-walk

Placed on a small hill, the impressive and quirky Edelcrantz octagonal tower was built in 1796 by Abraham Niclas Edelcrantz (1754–1821), who was a true Renaissance man. One of the original 18 members of the Swedish Academy (that today chooses the laureates for the Nobel Prize in literature), Edelcrantz was also head of the Royal Theatre, private secretary to the king, a celebrated poet, translator, and member of parliament. As an inventor, he was instrumental in the instigation of industrialism in Sweden.

His love life was less of a success. After unsuccessfully proposing to the Anglo-Irish author Maria Edgeworth (1768–1849), Edelcrantz remained heartbroken, unmarried and childless, spending much time ruminating in his octagonal creation.

One of his innovations, drawing on earlier work by the French inventor Claude Chappe (1763–1805), was the Swedish optical telegraph. It was inaugurated in 1794, when a birthday greeting (a poem written by Edelcrantz) for King Gustav III was transmitted from Katarina Church in Södermalm to the king's castle in Drottningholm. The Swedish telegraph was almost twice as fast as its French counterpart and later proved highly useful in the 1808 war against Russia. Telegraph stations were located around 10 km apart, and the octagonal tower served as one such station.

It also had many other functions: The high windows on the bottom floor were intended to allow sunlight to enter the orangery housed there, where delicate plants from the southern hemisphere were kept during the cold Swedish winters. The upper floor was Edelcrantz private dwelling place, and the roof had a viewing platform where the optical telegraph stood.

The style of architecture has been described as an original mixture of south-European classicism and north-European Gothic style. The latter could be seen first and foremost in the pointed-arch balusters of the balconies and terrace. In later times, however, these sadly were replaced with more neutral-looking balusters.

| | |
|---|---|
| 1897 Exposition | 249 |
| 92 Bloodbath stones | 40 |
| Airshafts of the Kronoberg remand prison | 116 |
| Alchemical ammunition? | 35 |
| Alley under St Eriksbron | 182 |
| Almgren factory | 88 |
| Anckarström's guns in the Royal Armoury | 34 |
| Anthroposophical library | 172 |
| Aronsberg Jewish cemetery | 104 |
| Bakery only sells their products to properly registered churches … | 79 |
| Barack Obama's bathroom | 289 |
| Bååtska palatset | 272 |
| Bellman House | 84 |
| Beware! | 29 |
| Biological museum | 252 |
| Black Friars' cellar | 24 |
| Black masses of Baron Jacques | 143 |
| Budo Zen Center | 192 |
| Burnt Lot | 28 |
| Cannon-flanked door of Västerlånggatan 68 | 16 |
| Cannonball in the wall | 44 |
| Captain Rolla monument | 82 |
| Captive viking statue | 260 |
| Carl Eldh studio museum | 204 |
| Cave and pump shaft at Haga Park | 218 |
| Chinese pavilion at Haga Park | 216 |
| Collective House | 114 |
| Copper faces of Rådhuset | 118 |
| Cracks of the bell of Katarina Church | 76 |
| Cross from the secretive order Arla Coldinu | 269 |
| Crossed-out Plommenfelt family crest | 58 |
| DC-3 79001 Hugin memorial stone | 254 |
| Decoration of the copper doors of Östgötagatan 14 | 74 |
| Devil, treasures and ghosts | 163 |
| 'Devil's bible' in the Royal Library | 278 |
| Draymen's guild rooms | 32 |
| Eastman Institute | 176 |
| Edelcrantz octagonal tower | 298 |
| Education of an originally proletarian neighborhood | 191 |
| Emanuel Swedenborg, Sweden's foremost mystic | 264 |
| Ersta communion wafer bakery | 78 |
| Exceptional eco system | 147 |
| Eye on Filmhuset | 238 |
| Faun and vulva ornament | 12 |
| Fenixplatset | 130 |
| Filmstaden | 232 |
| Firefighting museum | 73 |
| First-generation phone booth | 48 |
| Fiskartorpet | 296 |
| Five basic solides and sacred geometry | 286 |
| Flies' Meeting: where the city's latrines were emptied | 15 |
| Former Czechoslovakian Embassy | 280 |
| Föreningen för Fäktkonstens Främjande (FFF) | 194 |
| Freemason flag | 273 |
| Freemasonry in Sweden | 273 |
| Garden of the senses | 178 |
| Gåsgränd | 54 |
| Ghost castle's collection | 162 |
| Ghostly knocks of Colonel Gustavsson, the son of King Gustav III? | 65 |
| Giant's cauldron | 213 |
| Giraffe crane | 266 |
| Grave of Pompe | 184 |
| Haga Castle ruin | 220 |
| Hagalundsparken water tower | 224 |
| Hagströmer medico-historical library | 210 |
| Haunted basement | 55 |
| Haunting ghost? | 137 |
| Hey Alley | 56 |
| Hidden treasures of the Royal Institute of Technology | 288 |
| Huset Kronan | 50 |
| Inscription in the Brunkebergstunneln | 154 |
| Interior of St Görans gymnasium | 106 |
| Iron boy sculpture | 38 |
| Italian cultural institute | 240 |
| JAS 39 Gripen crash memorial | 94 |
| Jägarghyddan | 258 |
| Jugendstil doors of Gasverket | 124 |
| Julius Hus | 70 |
| Kaknäs pet cemetery | 236 |
| Karlberg runestone | 188 |
| Katarina Church and the history of witchcraft in Sweden | 77 |
| Katarina fire station lantern | 72 |
| Kronoberg Jewish burial site | 105 |
| Kungsträdgården metro station | 144 |
| Legend of the *Codex Gigas* | 279 |
| Lilla Hornsberg | 102 |
| Lodge of the Knights Templar | 160 |
| Many Queen Christina sites | 209 |
| Mårten Trotzigs gränd | 20 |
| Medusa head in Riddarholmskyrkan | 64 |

Mermaid statues at the Van der Noot Palace 92

Messenger pigeon club 206

Miniature replica of Mickes Serier, CD & vinyl 96

Miraculous silver image 25

Monica Zetterlund Park 196

Montelius grave 222

Murder in a church 65

Museum of Pharmaceutical History 126

National witch of Sweden 225

Old public urinal 36

Olle Olsson house museum 228

Origin of the racing pigeon's amazing capacity 207

Other orders at Piperska Muren 123

Owls of Ugglevikskällan 294

Par Bricole: a humorous order 87

Petrified cat bas-relief 52

Phantom statue 140

Piperska Muren garden 122

Place of quietude 179

Place to secretly store the country's gold reserve? 247

Plaque of Carl Larsson's birthplace 22

Poem for a dog 185

Queen Christina's gazebo 208

R1 292

Reimersholme vodka benches 98

Relief of Huset Brasan 26

Reliefs of Centralposthuset 138

Reliefs of Centrumhuset 132

Rent Westerdahl's historical living quarters 71

Rose door 30

Röda Rummet at Berns 150

Rune stone corner 46

Sabbatsbergs Kyrka 180

Scratch with the diamond ring 61

Secret of Adelswärd House 142

Secrets of Kastellholmen 268

Site of the first theatre with plays in Swedish 39

Skandia cinema 128

Skanstull cholera graveyard 68

Skånska Gruvan 244

Slides of the old National Archive 62

St Matteus parish library 190

Stairs of Centrumhuset 135

Stockholm Bloodbath of 1520 42

Stolen child 15

Stone of the High Council 186

Storytelling room 170

Submerged shipwrecks 269

Suicide to avoid disability ... 177

Sven Hedin's house 110

Swedenborg Church 156

Swedenborg's gazebo 262

Swedenborg's teaching 158

Teater dur och moll 80

Tekniska Högskolan metro station 282

The Family statue's rotating feature 14

'The head gardener must know that the planets and the 12 signs of the zodiac should correspond in seeding and planting work.' 257

Trip to France to steal industrial secrets 89

Turkish kiosk 214

Two other replicas of the gazebo 263

Ugglan Pharmacy 136

Unique acoustics 155

Vestiges of the former Biograf Draken cinema 108

Victoriaväxhuset 200

Viking ship at the former school of naval warfare 270

Villa Bellona 198

Villa Lusthusporten 242

Vodka King's occultist daughters 99

Was Descartes Poisoned by a Catholic priest? 18

Wasa garden 256

'We have plenty of time, just for you' 191

What is anthroposophy? 174

What is left of the exposition? 251

What is the Coldinu Order? 123

Winner of the Kasper Salin prize 284

Wittrock Tower 202

Zetterlund's hairdresser 197

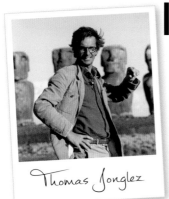

Thomas Jonglez

I t was September 1995 and Thomas Jonglez was in Peshawar, the northern Pakistani city 20 kilometres from the tribal zone he was to visit a few days later. It occurred to him that he should record the hidden aspects of his native city, Paris, which he knew so well. During his seven-month trip back home from Beijing, the countries he crossed took in Tibet (entering clandestinely, hidden under blankets in an overnight bus), Iran and Kurdistan. He never took a plane but travelled by boat, train or bus, hitchhiking, cycling, on horseback or on foot, reaching Paris just in time to celebrate Christmas with the family.

On his return, he spent two fantastic years wandering the streets of the capital to gather material for his first "secret guide", written with a friend. For the next seven years he worked in the steel industry until the passion for discovery overtook him. He launched Jonglez Publishing in 2003 and moved to Venice three years later.

In 2013, in search of new adventures, the family left Venice and spent six months travelling to Brazil, via North Korea, Micronesia, the Solomon Islands, Easter Island, Peru and Bolivia.

After seven years in Rio de Janeiro, he now lives in Berlin with his wife and three children.

Jonglez Publishing produces a range of titles in nine languages, released in 40 countries.